COPPERNICKEL

number 22 / spring 2016

EDITOR/MANAGING EDITOR
Wayne Miller

EDITORS: POETRY
Brian Barker
Nicky Beer

EDITOR: FICTION & NONFICTION
Joanna Luloff

EDITOR: FICTION
Teague Bohlen

SENIOR EDITORS
Steven Dawson
Emily Jessen

ASSOCIATE EDITORS
Angela Bogart-Monteith
Jacqueline Gallegos
Meredith Herndon
Jennifer Loyd
Lyn Poats
Kyra Scrimgeour
Carley Tacker

EDITORIAL INTERNS
Karl Chwe
Sammi Johnson

ASSISTANT EDITORS
Joseph Carrillo
Bri Galanaugh
Libby Gemperline
Jack Gialanella
Hannah Miles
Kevin Nagle
Kristine Oakhurst
Paige Perich

Jake
Cele
Tristi
Grac
Benja

CONTRIBUTING EDITORS
Robert Archambeau
Mark Brazaitis
Geoffrey Brock
A. Papatya Bucak
Victoria Chang
Martha Collins
Robin Ekiss
Tarfia Faizullah
V. V. Ganeshananthan
Kevin Haworth
Joy Katz
David Keplinger
Jesse Lee Kercheval
Jason Koo
Thomas Legendre
Randall Mann
Adrian Matejka
Pedro Ponce
Kevin Prufer
Frederick Reiken
James Richardson
Emily Ruskovich
Eliot Khalil Wilson

ART CONSULTANTS
Maria Elena Buszek
Adam Lerner

OFFICE MANAGERS
Francine Olivas-Zarate
Tamara Romero

Copper Nickel is the national literary journal housed at the University of Colorado Denver. Published in March and September, it features poetry, fiction, essays, and work in translation by established and emerging writers. We welcome submissions from all writers. Submissions are assumed to be original and unpublished. For more information, please visit **copper-nickel.org**. Subscriptions are available—and at discounted rates for students—at regonline.com/coppernickelsubscriptions. *Copper Nickel* is distributed to subscribers and through Publishers Group West and Media Solutions, as well as digitally catalogued by EBSCO. We are deeply grateful for the support of the Department of English and the College of Liberal Arts & Sciences at the University of Colorado Denver.

CONTENTS

FEATURE

FICTION

NONFICTION

POETRY

TRANSLATION FOLIOS

On the Cover / Christine Stormberg, *Samy*, Oil on canvas, 2009

(for more about Christine Stormberg's work
visit christinestormberg.com)

Editor's Note:

WE AT COPPER NICKEL ARE very excited to announce the Jake Adam York Prize in poetry for a first or second book—a collaboration between *Copper Nickel* and Milkweed Editions.

We will begin accepting submissions of first or second book-length poetry manuscripts via the *Copper Nickel* website in July of 2016, and the final due date for submission will be October 15, 2016. The winner will receive $2,000, and Milkweed Editions will publish the winning manuscript in April of 2018 under a standard royalty contract.

We're particularly thrilled to announce that the inaugural judge for the prize will be Ross Gay, author of three poetry collections, most recently *Catalog of Unabashed Gratitude*, which was a finalist for the National Book Award and, as of this writing, is currently a finalist for the National Book Critics Circle Award.

Our goal in instituting the Jake Adam York Prize is to honor Jake's name and legacy with a top-tier book prize that will offer to the winning poet not just publication but also high-quality design, marketing, and strong national distribution. Milkweed—which has an excellent marketing and design team and distributes through Publishers Group West—can offer all of these things.

Prize entrants will receive a *Copper Nickel* subscription in exchange for their $25 reading fee, and any money left over after production costs have been covered will go toward paying *Copper Nickel* contributors—something we plan to start doing in 2017.

We're very excited about these developments!

AND WE'RE ALSO VERY EXCITED about the issue you have in front of you—so before we get ahead of ourselves, please lean back and enjoy.

—Wayne Miller

SEQUOIA NAGAMATSU

The Rest of the Way

COMPANION

ON OUR WEDDING DAY, you weighed 115 lbs. When you died, you weighed 97. You are now 8.7 cups of ash, and I figure I can make enough 1:25 scale figurines of you from what you've left behind, so we can see the world.

In Tochigi Prefecture, there's a theme park called Tobu World Square where 140,000 miniature figurines are sightseeing at famous landmarks. A boy holds a balloon at the base of the Statue of Liberty. A young couple strolls the gardens of Versailles toward the New York City skyline, toying with the idea of making love behind a carefully manicured privet hedge. An elderly man reads a map as he rests in the shadow of the Parthenon. He's smiling. Perhaps because he's saved up for this trip his entire life. Or maybe he taught seventh grade history for over thirty years, and this is the first time he's been able to see the world outside of a textbook.

I try to capture you laughing. But you're angry sometimes, too. Eyebrows raised. Arms crossed. Airports always brought the worst out in us like the time I lost hundreds of dollars playing slots during a Las Vegas layover. Or the time you brought a flight attendant to tears because she demanded that we check our carry-ons even though we had room under the seat. I'm painting your favorite blue dress on now. The one with little pink flowers. Your travel dress. Elegant. Lightweight. The shawl my mother knitted is draped over your shoulders. Your mouth is pursed, and I imagine us standing in line somewhere. I'll make a figure of myself with an arm reaching out, rubbing your back. Or maybe I'll be flipping through a travel guide, talking about a starred restaurant, oblivious to your frustrations. *You said:* "How can you not be bothered by this?" And glared at a would-be line cutter wearing an I <3 NY sweatshirt. "I'm going to the bathroom. You better not let anybody cut in front of us."

NARITA

YOU GLANCE AT A young Australian man talking to his mate. He's muscular and tan, and probably surfs every chance he gets. I glance at a pale brunette with headphones on, sitting by the gate. Stand-by. English maybe. Black stockings. Listening to what?

Classical, Jazz, heavy metal hair bands? You take my hand unexpectedly as we approach the jet bridge. I smile stupidly at the girl taking my ticket. You notice. We haven't had sex in two months, and when I tried to join you in the shower one night, you jumped out and said we should take a trip somewhere.

There's no room for our figurines at Tobu's Narita exhibit. Only a few model 747s being loaded with luggage, the terminals, and the tarmac busy with service vehicles. But I carve us anyway and imagine us—at security, buying magazines, arguing at the ticket counter, holding hands after we've taken our seats. You leaned over me to peer through the window as the plane took off. Your perfume smelled like cinnamon and honey, and I wanted to kiss your neck. *I said:* "I think we needed this trip."

Angkor Wat

After the guided tour, we explored the complex on our own, wandering through the corridors of the lower levels, which represent the underworld, and up to the highest stupas where paradise and enlightenment awaits. Tourists streamed around us, clicking cameras, carelessly wielding parasols. We maneuvered around photographers—*sumimasen, sumimasen.* Stopped to press a button on a lone traveler's point-and-shoot. But here, there is just us. I quickly place our figures just outside of one of the gates before anyone sees me step over the rope. A few feet of bonsai tree jungle separates Cambodia from the Great Wall of China.

You are pointing at the tree line where I've placed a die-cast Macaque holding a Louis Vuitton handbag the size of a button. I am running after the monkey, frozen mid-sprint a few inches from him. You had put your bag down for a moment to take a photo of a purple flower growing out of a relief when you noticed the tiny robber creeping closer. You told me to look at the monkey. *Kawaii*, you said and pointed your camera at him. *You screamed:* "The monkey has my purse!"

I ran. The men within earshot ran, as the Macaque climbed the temple walls. He sat perched under the giant, stone lip of a Buddha and opened his mouth wide, as if to mock us, exposing his sharp canines. One of the men tried to entice him with a power bar. "Come down here you piece of shit," I cried. I began climbing the wall. Tried to anyway. But one of the tour guides grabbed my shoulder and pulled me off. *You said:* "Let it go. It's gone." You collapsed next to a sculpture of Vishnu, protector of the world and God of universal order. *I said:* We can replace it. But you explained they didn't make that one anymore.

Taj Mahal

No one told us about the crowds and the smell of feet and the beggars and the never ending cycle of getting ripped off by drivers and "official" guides, although we knew, in a theoretical sense, crowds and poverty were part of the fabric of India. The clerk at our hotel in Delhi gave us a corner room for my Hokkaido Fighters hat. A man on a scooter snatched your head scarf as he drove by, nearly pulling you to the ground. A young boy on a moped chased after the thief but lost him in the thickness of Agra. Debarshi. Twelve-years-old. He had a sick mother (we wanted to believe he had a sick mother). You wanted to give him as many rupees we could spare. And as I guarded you while you fished through your belt bag, we both noticed the boy fixating on my shoes, the fact that his feet were bare, dry and cracked as the ground beneath him. We looked at each other, and your eyes said: take off your shoes. And I did without hesitation. I laced the boy up and walked bare foot the rest of the afternoon, feeling India hot against my skin until another boy sold me a pair of sandals. We walked side-by-side, holding each other like we used to in high school, following a man who said he knew a scenic route to the Red Gate.

Of course, at Tobu, none of this exists. There is only the Taj Mahal, the monument of a man's love for his wife. I place our figurines in the vast, manicured garden under the shade of a tree. Here, we are frozen in the conversation we had that afternoon. And I wish we would have stayed there longer, that I would have fought harder, so everything that happened after would cease to be. *You said:*

"Do you think we have that kind of love?

At first I thought we were talking about the architectural wonder behind us but then realized you were staring at a young couple kissing passionately near the reflecting pool.

"Isn't everyone like that at first?"

"We weren't."

"I'm pretty sure we were."

"High school," you said.

"So the first few years we knew each other doesn't count?" I asked.

"Do you think it's possible to really know what you want when you're that young?"

"And what do you want now?"

"Not this," you said, standing up.

"And this trip?"

"I guess," you began. You stared at the pink, floral flip-flops beside me, my dirty feet, digging into the lawn. "I guess this is a test. To see if there's anything."

I didn't prod any further. I nodded. I said we should get going if we wanted to make it back to the hotel. I could have asked how I was faring. I could have said more.

The guide who came with us had disappeared by the time we returned to the gate. We walked fast, ignoring the flank of panhandlers, guides, and vendors, opting instead to find a reliable rickshaw driver that could take us to the train station. A clean-cut man with a Freddie Mercury mustache waved us over. We were so focused on him, on his unusually shiny carriage, and on getting back to our room that we didn't see what was coming. We no longer walked side-by-side. You walked ahead. You took the first step into the street.

SPHINX

AND I WOULD HAVE made you take photos of me, crushing the Sphinx with my fingers, nibbling on the beast's backside. There would have been other people, other couples taking similar photos, making the most of the perspective from an observation point. You would tell me I was getting ripped off by a man trying to rent us camels. You would tell me that you really could care less about the damn camels. On a tour we would learn about secret chambers built beneath the Sphinx that remain a mystery. And before I even spoke, you would tell me aliens aren't the answer to everything. But what if, what if? My figurine's arms wave wildly. Your figurine looks annoyed, is looking off into the distance where smog meets sand, where the shanties of Cairo punctuate the horizon.

COLOSSEUM

DESPITE ARGUING FOR MOST of the plane ride, we would make up at the bed and break-fast you picked out, kissing to a peek-a-boo view of St. Peter's Basilica. We would stay in, forgetting about the Segway tour we signed up for (that I signed up for). You would say that it didn't matter that I forgot the travel plan binder you had been putting together for a month, that we would let spontaneity carry us. Maybe you would have said that. Possibly. Or you would have said there was no point dwelling on it, that we would have to make do. Maybe you would have called your sister and told her to go to our apartment, so she could read off your airtight itinerary. We would waste half the day waiting. We wouldn't have time to go inside the Colosseum before it closed, wouldn't see where gladiators waited for their death or glory, where tigers and rhinos would rise to the arena for a hunt. But we would stroll outside of its arches after dining at a Michelin starred rooftop restaurant across the way—Aroma—with two glasses of rosé each.

At Tobu (and in Rome), the Colosseum is awash in gold instead of white light, which means somewhere, someone's death sentence has been commuted or rescinded.

Or capital punishment has been abolished in some province or country. I place us beside a lamppost near where the Arch of Constantine would be. My arm is around your waist. You're looking up, pointing. I'm looking right at you.

EIFFEL

I WOULD HAVE SAID: If you really want to go up there. You would have said: I wouldn't feel like I really experienced Paris if we didn't. We would go in the morning, before the queues got too long, before the forecast brought fog and rain. We would stop on the first level and have an overpriced brunch brought in a picnic basket. I would say: at least drinks were included. I would say: It better not rain when we get up there. I would say: Even though this place is such a romantic cliché, I'm incredibly happy to be here with you. I would say: I love you.

Even at 1:25 scale, the tower is too tall for me to reach the top, so I place us on the balcony of the first level looking out at the New York City skyline with a pair of binoculars. But we would take the lift to the cupola soon after, drink tourist-bait champagne, and ask a Bulgarian man to take our photo twice. First shot: Both of us side-by-side, smiling at the camera. Second shot: Staring into each other's eyes. You crinkling your nose. Me stroking your hair. We would hang the photos in the living room.

TWIN TOWERS

WE WERE SLEEPING WHILE it happened. I turned on the television while you prepared breakfast. Got ready for work. Tied the new silk tie you bought at the mall the day before. You said: Oh my god, look! You said: America. I said nothing. I watched the headlines scroll across the screen and sipped on the miso you had warmed. You said: That was on our itinerary; we were going to go to the observation deck. You said: Those people. We canceled our trip that year. There would be another time—later, after all this. You asked: Do we know anyone in New York?

At Tobu, there's a plaque next to the World Trade Center (1973 – 2001). I place us in a crosswalk adjacent to the south tower. We are surrounded by power suits, fanny packs, taxis, and delivery men carrying packages. A woman walks her dog. A couple tries to find themselves on a map. A homeless man sits on a bench. I don't know what day or what time it is in this snap shot of New York. A few minutes before the first crash? Seconds? Or is it years or decades? But like our conversation at the Taj Mahal, the next moment will never be. I say: Let's catch a Broadway show. I ask: Do you know where you're going?

TOBU FORGETS THE SIDE streets, the parking lots, and the slums surrounding world landmarks. Every exhibit is a postcard. And while I want time to stand still at the Taj Mahal, I cannot forget.

In our bedroom I've recreated it, the Agra streets filled with dust and traffic and the cacophony of vendors and hustlers. The shiny rickshaw that would have taken us to the train station. A boy who tugged on my shirt. Our figurines are on the edge of the street. You are stepping forward, waving to the driver. Not far away, a man is selling balloons attached to a cart on his bicycle. The balloons along with a stereo blaring music camouflage the approaching bus and the two mopeds speeding alongside it. I've created everybody here in a variety of poses. The balloon man who tried to warn you, waving his arms. You on the ground with your eyes closed. Me holding you to my chest, wailing for help. Me pulling you away from harm, as the bus plowed through the crowded street. I would have asked: Are you okay? And you would have said: I think so. I would have squeezed you so hard then, kissed you. And you would have let me. The driver would take us to the train station and you would rest your head on my shoulders. And I would have said: Maybe that was a test. And we would say other things, too. But not for a while. Not until we got back home. We would remain silent the rest of the way.

JASWINDER BOLINA

Epistemic Love Poem

> If there were a verb meaning "to believe falsely,"
> it would not have any significant first-person
> present indicative.
> —Ludwig Wittgenstein,
> *Philosophical Investigations*

In Crimea now the larks might be muzzled by artillery
and crap weather, how should I know? In Haifa now
the guns must be running, I have no idea. In Kobani,
a boy is waxing a Kalashnikov. A boy is waning
in a blood puddle, I don't know. I'm not in Missouri.
I'm not in Humboldt Park or Harlem. I'm here with you,
wrought simple and plain happy. The only city I know
is your city, is your city block, your boulevard between
the German bar and the orthodontist's. The only city
I know is the square of sidewalk your shadow paints.
Everywhere else is switched off now, every current
stilled, the Gulf Stream is in sleep mode, its porpoises
unplugged, its seagulls powered down now dangling
from clouds that are stuck static in their full upright
and locked positions. No carbon is there baking
the human sky, no Ebola, no typhoon churning.
No Obama is there in his white office, no Mitch
McConnell in the garret of his own braincase, no pope
infallible, no lama enlightened, no ayatollah knows
what I know now I know you, and no, I don't call you
darling. I don't call you *honey* or *sugar* or *babe*,
those names made for other bodies, those noises made
lame by other people, and the other bodies are switched off
now slack mannequins on trolley cars, in Hondas, in jets
stopped over Crimea, over Kobani and Haifa, everyone
dumbstruck everywhere still as a book on a shelf.
If it isn't written by you, I won't read it. If it isn't about you,

I won't know it, and I won't call you *bunny* or *sweetheart*
or *pumpkin* now I know you are my wild earthquake,
my ontological kazoo, my dizzy robin of ghost feathers,
your voice is a brontosaur. It's bigger than everything.
Your mind is bigger than mine, it frightens me,
but I kiss your shins and shoulders now, I kiss your hips,
it's like kissing rainwater though I know now no rain
exists if it isn't kissing your face. I'm being ridiculous,
I know! But my chest is a rowboat rolled over and over.
My chest is a boulder, the boulder crashed through
the floodlight of my chest, and I believe falsely now
no horror exists. I believe falsely no other joy exists.
I believe now in every love song. Every love song
is wrong that doesn't know you, my transcendental
tea cup, my butter knife in a light socket, you are my
space plane, my only space plane. I do dare to eat a peach.
I do dare disturb the universe, and if the universe turns out
to be a simulation, if the universe is a false front or a figment
of a dog's eye in another universe, I don't need to know now
I know you I don't know and I don't need know.

Wedding Poem

Is it your fallout shelter? Is it your diesel generator?
Is it the truth in your pamphlets: your incontrovertible
alien and undeniable sasquatch? Is it your stockpile
of Spam and ammo or the campfire's gleam crinkling
in the dome of your aluminum hat that so beguiles me?
Woe, those Saskatchewan nights I huddled without you,
my camera on a hair trigger, my motion sensors tensing.
I listened for your ghost dogs baying in the hollows,
for your poltergeist banging in my barn loft.
I waited for your landing lights to ignite my tree line,
your tractor beam to come abduct, dissect, and erase me.
Those years alone with my Ouija board, I pleaded
for you to hijack my airwaves, to come invade
my Winnebago. Come bodysnatch me! I demanded
the simple proof of you, for your puff of smoke drifted
over my grassy knoll, your Freemasons peeking
into my Bohemian Grove, but the specter of you,
I couldn't capture, so no one believed me. Your signals
in the noise, I couldn't decipher, and no one believed me.
Nobody ever believed me until you believed me.
Now, my skull and bones inducted into the conspiracy
of your company, your Opus Dei inviting my Illuminati,
now you are real, so I am real. Now, shudders the zombie
night, the end is nigh, only you believe me, so divvy up
the jerky, my heart. Ration out the trail mix, my one
and only. I'll bolt the cellar door, you load the crossbows.
I have no idea what happens next.

LAUREN MOSELEY

New Marriage

For years I pronounced *timbre* like *timber*.
You pointed out the difference
weeks after our wedding

and I imagined the sound a maple makes
when it sings without strings stretched over its body.

It is not pitch, not volume,
but something deep inside the sound
that quivers.

My deepest fear:

that one day I won't be able to stand
the sight of you, the sound of your voice.

The maple chopped, stripped, sawed, and sanded.

You pick up the old guitar,
the one you got from a pawn shop before we met,
when we both were wild.

You play the same verse over and over,
changing a note each time, and it does get better.

Sitting in this cluttered room,
among objects that fill me with love
and revulsion for their familiarity,

the plain present strikes me like an ax.

There could have been so many versions of us,
why this one?

If we are to survive, we must be different people together,
a little different every day.

The ax in my side softens as you begin to sing.

ELYSE FENTON

Empire

Across history, courtyard swans
knit their tongues from fallen skeins

of blood. Before they built the Great Wall
they built the idea of the Great Wall.

So great the workers' bodies would fit
ambered inside with their bootlaces

and spines intact as the border between
two warring countries. The blindness

comes only after the spangling darkness
wears down, a neckful of light drained

from the wings and jagged snapped-off
beaks of the swans prying at the ancient

masonry for a kernel, a button, a fist
broken in the shape of a swan.

DAVID KEPLINGER

Magic

In the padlocked trunk before they dropped him
in the river, Houdini was said to foresee
his mother's death. Stuck in his box, at the end
of a chain, he felt the death, its approach,
her worry growing smaller at the eyes as she

removed herself from herself, her body shrunken
to the size of a keyhole. I believe that grief
can travel distances like that. My mother's
cough would wake me up at night, two hundred
miles away. That was a year ago, before she

got too small. She drowned in a cloud
of bright white baby hair. She lay on the bed,
flat on her back, the last I saw her, still and calm.
Then truly as if a lever were pulled, she tipped
backwards, out of view.

ANDREA READ

Retrato de Viuda con Caballero Andante

My husband departed one spring

        right out the kitchen window.

Back soon, he says,

     fastening his armor.

Ok, I say.   Now off

     he goes. I wait

          and wait. Winter arrives. Snow falls

     for months. No, for years. By this time

       I am asleep

             on a glacier.

Ok, finally

      I wake up.   *Yoohoo—*

   nothing happens—not a sound.

So

I tidy up the place, rebuild the shed, the chicken coop,

take up needlepoint, tire of it, think

                                        Wait! why

        waste my time
                        with housework when in winter

        it's birds everywhere!

Cardinals, bullfinches, blackbirds out my kitchen window—

        there they go   defending territory
attracting mates.

I memorize medieval ballads—knights riding up on horseback,

                        home from the war. In each one

the husband is unfamiliar, unrecognizable. Or

                unrecognized.   Big difference.

Here's Catalina, seated under a laurel,

        next to a stream. She's daydreaming, watching the water

                and this knight rides by (slowly) on his horse, her reverie

broken. She flags him down—

        Have you seen my husband? No, no haven't seen him—what's

he look like? Oh he's tall and blond, handsome like you, etc.

Ah yes, he was killed by a coronel. Asked me to marry you in his place.

       (tricky bastard—I think he's cracked

a smile)

       Oh no, I would never marry you, not in seven years, never! I'd sooner

          send my daughters to the convent and my sons to the king.

    She sounds serious.

In most versions of the ballad

       she resists the knight's advance.   But!   here comes

what's always troubled me—the husband reveals himself

       in the last stanza, calls her

by name

          Calla, calla, Catalina
          Calla, calla de una vez,
          Que estás hablando con tu marido
          Y no lo sabes reconocer
          Que estás hablando con tu marido
          Y no lo sabes reconocer.

Damn,   so all along

       it was a test—look

how he sneaks his way

       back in through the window. But guess what

I finally figured out, she knew all along
              it was him.

So anyway, spring comes. I ready the flower beds. I plant

          peonies, snapdragons, creeping

thyme. The neighbors take pity

                  when they see me alone in the garden, bring

pot roast, casseroles, cherry cobbler. At the bar

they meet for cocktails, hash over my widowhood—

          they relish this topic. Husbands offer

                  to fix my roof, and the plumbing. I don't tell them

I've begun to hear you whistling to me

from far away, after nightfall

                    like some ovenbird

flying over the forest canopy.

When you finally arrive and I'm seated under a tree,

say, the apple, or the white oak (my favorite)

and you ride up on your horse, and you take off your armor

I'll ask you for news of my husband—

how romantic

would that be.

Son in This Story the Oaks Are Tremendous

There are forests that follow rivers
of legendary strength and beauty

become lost in mist,
cloud forests.

So the first question
is what lost means.

Your orders came today.
You ship out

in the fall. Lost is now
another kind of question.

I will tell the family
you are cold and afraid.

I will tell the family
you have just reached out
and touched your own
story, as if it were
your own manhood.

How We Manage Since Father Died

We have a finch.
Her name is Lucy.
She is a mature deity.

We dress her
in brown leather shoes
and handmade woolens.
We cling to her.

The village has fled insomnia—
some of us hunt,
some weave dresses of yak hair,
others persist in finding a detour.

I've pitched my tent
on the bank of the river,
here, where it bends
to the left then folds

gently in a different direction.
It is a protective river—
a catastrophic river.

I cover myself in pitch
I weave grass through my teeth

I have almost
spent myself

Twelve more hours—
father is nearly
                    soil

HENRY ISRAELI

The Fathers Show No Mercy

1.

From the limber branches of the willow hang
the beards of the fathers.
From the damp soil grow
the arms of the fathers.
Under our pillows where we tuck our hands we find
the fragile knees of the fathers.
Behind the sofas, among the dust balls and gum wrappers,
the lips of the fathers.
Under spare tires in car trunks, the fingers.
In the ashes and the settling embers of the fireplace,
the tongues, the ears, the etcetera.

2.

The fathers are not in heaven.
They search for their names
in the trash piles of the city.
They hold the keys to the kingdom
in the black purses
beneath their eyes.
One day they will give us
our bread and it will be
filled with their teeth.
We will beg their forgiveness
but they will only smile
their crooked, broken smiles.
They will never lay down
their hammers for they
have work to do, plans that began

before we were born—and they
have been sleeping far too long.

3.

Look! An orchid stands up tall
and walks across the garden

The fathers are sick with delight.

ALICIA LAI

Divine

Our gods study psychotherapy. Our gods
Freudian slip. Our gods build their homes
on the outskirts of town to save
on commuting. Our gods aren't so great.
Our gods chug cereal. They lip
at the snow, consuming
everything. Our gods live in a maniacal universe:
an urban street corner of punk
rock. The material parts of them can be bought.
Everyone tells me this. But our gods like the ragtag life
and the street-swollen swagger, flinging gangster shadow
puppets. Our gods are the Divine O.G., backwards
or not. Our gods are whole and full and
secular. Sometimes they are sullen.
Our gods always win the human
race. Our gods left a gun in the safe. Our gods
handed me the combination on a Post-it. How volatile
they are. See, our gods have artificial
intelligence exponentially larger than ours. This is how
they understand the choices we think
we have. Sometime in the night, our gods told
the DJ to hype up the beat, and one
god pushed the button.

Translation Folio

EMMANUEL MOSES

Translator's Introduction

Marilyn Hacker

EMMANUEL MOSES WAS BORN IN Casablanca in 1959, the son of a French-educated German Jew and a French Jew of Polish descent: one an historian of philosophy and the other a painter. He spent his early childhood in France, lived from the age of ten until his mid-twenties in Israel, where he studied history at the Hebrew University of Jerusalem, and then returned to Paris, where he still lives. He is the author of twelve collections of poems—these translations are from the most recent, *Sombre comme le temps*, published by Gallimard in 2014—as well as a writer of novels and short fiction. Fluent in four languages, Moses is a translator into French of contemporary Hebrew fiction and poetry, notably of Yehuda Amichai and David Grossman; he edited anthologies of modern Hebrew poetry in translation for the publishers Obsidiane and Gallimard. He also translates from the German and from the English, including poems by C.K. Williams, Raymond Carver, and Gabriel Levin, and some of my own work.

The three poems here all consider permanence and vulnerability focusing on the insubstantiality of what seems at first most solid: a house, a wall, a row of stones. But all the possible, impermanent histories of such structures are implied. A wall can protect or exclude. A house can be abandoned or destroyed. Its inhabitants can be forced out, evicted or deported, with all that that implies both in the history of the Jews in Europe and in the history of Israel and Palestine. An ephemeral seeming object— a mailbox with a name plate— survives its use and becomes a kind of memorial to the disappeared. Meditation on history is itself part of a meta-narrative of dialogue, or a longing for dialogue, with the dead, here, the poet's father, the historian Stéphane Moses, who died in 2007 and who remains an interlocutor in his son's work.

A polyglot whose experience of the world comes as much from travel and human intercourse as from books, from an interrogation of the past which coexists with his experience of the present, Emmanuel Moses is a kind of Poète sans frontières. While some contemporary French poets eschew geographical specificity, a perennial subject of Moses' poems is the crossing and the porosity of actual borders, geographical and temporal. A (Proustian?) train of thought set in motion by the placement of a park bench, the stripe of sunlight on a brick wall, will move the speaker and the poem itself from Paris to Jerusalem, from a boyhood memory to a 19th century chronicle, from Stendhal to Stalingrad.

Yet, despite his multilingual erudition, the range of his interlocutors, and his obvious pleasure (not in the least doctrinal) in formal experimentation, Moses is a poet with a direct and almost intimate address to the reader who engages with his work: in turn wry, melancholy, funny, self-deprecating, mercurial, fraternal.

(Another translation of a poem by Emanuel Moses from the same collection can be read at http://plumepoetry.com/2014/10/she-painted-artichokes/.)

Stones

Revere a wall and it becomes venerable
There are those who refuse to understand that
I'm not defending idolatry
But thoughts and prayers transform the things they address
Incantations changed the giant stones called megaliths
Dolmens, menhirs, cairns
Aligned as at Stonehenge
No cave would be sacred without someone seeking transcendence
I'd discuss this with my father
We'd drink coffee, he'd be lying down or propped up in an armchair
I was always nervous
I had to prove something
Now I find him everywhere
Death bestows omnipresence
In death time is at last reversible
The field where galgals are lined up as far as the eye can see becomes my father's ghost
Am I the Prince of Denmark for all that?
I don't need a watchtower or a night patrol
Or black midnight
Sometimes I'd talk nonsense
The coffee was never strong enough
I dived into a whirlpool of dead men
Wholeheartedly
Wasting my time
And beyond the windowpane the sky was breathing
Insensible to our fates
Which was why I loved it
As a man might love a woman for her indifference

A House and a Wall

In front of this foundation, its rows of perbend stones thrusting up from the ground
Where grass still grows
In front of this germ of private life
In front of this absence already reeking of abandonment
How not to stop
Not muse and reflect
On what is after all
Like a strange entombment

"A wall always has two sides," said the worker
"A wall always has two sides," said the poet
"A wall only has one side," said the soldier
"A wall only has one side," said the politician
"A wall only has one side," said the villager
"Walls don't exist," said the prisoner
"Walls don't exist," said the child
"Walls don't exist," said the lovers

A house is born from no earth
No sky or stars
No trees
A house, one day, will be everything
You'll move in, you'll leave it
You'll be evicted, expelled, it will be illegally occupied
It will be paradise and hell
An ideal attained, a nightmare come to life

"I don't have time to die," says the living man
"I don't have time for resurrection," says the dead man
From the two sides of the wall
Two sides of the bones

The poet says "I saw that in my childhood—a house swallowed up
In the dark of night."
The dead man lights a cigarette—why not?
The living man coughs and spits on the mud that will be a floor or a wall

The dead man blows on his finger-bones laughing
The living man doesn't want to think about the plot of land before his eyes any more
The cigarette goes back and forth from the dead to the living, from the living to the dead
The poet will never climb the wall
Will never build a house
But he will eat up his life in cigarettes, love, dreams
Sick with time

Meditation

For Marcel Cohen

What happens to the letterboxes of demolished houses?
What do they do to perform their task whatever happens?
Because mail can continue to arrive
Sometimes even decades after it was posted
—I received a postcard today that my father wrote thirty-four years ago
With a picture of a nineteenth-century advertisement
"Waiter! An Inca Cola!"—
Sometimes they remain attached to a wall that holds up nothing but emptiness
That separates one emptiness from another
They age slowly
Rust, gape open, distorted like age-tormented faces
Always bravely displaying
The names of long-dead residents
Eternal addressees in brass or copper card-holders
Often the address has disappeared
If not the whole street, replaced by a newer, wider one
Or by a playground, a mall, a parking lot
But they continue to sport an air of being at the center of the world
And they're not altogether wrong in that
For nothingness is the secret heart of being
Brushing off the nonsense of the situation with a stoic's or a cynic's haughtiness
They contemplate the person passing by
Whom they invite to meditate on permanence and impermanence
The visible and the invisible
Time and space
Memory and forgetfulness
The person who tears them from their supports
To use them as decorations or sell them to the ironmonger
To throw them on the closest dump or keep them as souvenirs
Is like someone who uproots a strong-rooted tree
He digs a hole that never will be filled
He kills the dead a second time
Whose voices cry out from the empty depths.

Translated from the French by Marilyn Hacker

ASHLEY DAVIDSON

Zebra Creek

THE KING OAK STOOD AT the northeast corner of the Anderson farm, off the Marengo road. It was charred black by an old lightning strike, but still alive, and still the tallest tree in Half Moon Township. Mr. Anderson had told Ava so. From the very top, on a clear day, you could see fifty miles—two days travel—all the way to Bellefonte, the county seat.

Since the Andersons had taken her in, Ava had become a great captain of trees, tearing the hems from her dresses, running lines up her itchy woolen stockings, and the king oak was the proudest and stateliest of her fleet. Climbing was the only way to escape the Anderson children. Mrs. Anderson forbade them, her voice high and fluty like a possum's. A good way to break your neck.

Ava had only to slip a hand into the tree's rough armpit, and haul herself up, surveying the land below as from the mast of a ship: the Andersons' wheat fields, the sunlit glint of Half Moon Creek, and, in the distance, the blackened metal roof of what had, for a few months, been her family's rented house.

Place was a tinderbox, she'd heard Mr. Anderson say.

The king oak had twin trunks. A lovers' tree, the Anderson girls called it. They were pale, auburn-haired girls with wide-set eyes the color of weak tea. They skipped in rings around the base, chanting taunts up into the branches.

> *Ring around the oak patch*
> *Pocket full of matches*
> *Ashes, Ashes*
> *They all burn down*

Leaning forward, Ava caught flashes of dusty calico dresses through the leaves below. She counted, measuring the rhythm and speed of their revolutions, biting the insides of her cheeks, saliva pooling under her tongue. She lowered her chin, puckered, and released a carefully aimed filament. It fell just short of the girls' feet. Ava straightened, hugged the trunk, held her breath—not breathing was the secret to invisibility. The girls shrieked, kicked dust over the spit, and started a new song.

> *Luke and Ava sitting in a tree, k-i-s-s-i-n-g,*
> *First comes love, then comes marriage,*
> *Then comes a baby in a baby carriage.*

They attacked the backs of their hands with lurid smooching, twisting away from little Luke Anderson, who still had his milk teeth, laughing as they ran off. Left alone, Luke glared up at Ava like a small bloodthirsty dog.

She didn't feel like an orphan. Mr. Anderson was kind, the household lively. Before long, her parents would return from a trip with a packet of licorice. Her father had bought her licorice to cure the heartache of leaving the Parker place, where the cat had just kittened.

This was their chance to make something of their own, her father had said. She had been promised a kitten, but when it came time to leave they still hadn't opened their eyes and couldn't be separated from their mother.

•

THE MEN STARTED DIGGING. No climbing today, Mr. Anderson said. From the window, Ava could just make out the tops of the men's heads over the crest of the hill. The oak's bark had gone a wintry grey-brown, leafless branches buffeted by the cold gusts.

The Andersons had taken Ava in until a blood relative could be located. Before the fire, Ava's parents had been newcomers to the area, and inquires were slow.

"Where was it you were living before?" Mrs. Anderson asked again, question laced with sweet cunning.

"On Mr. Parker's farm," Ava said, though it was hard to remember the Parkers', where her father had been the hired man, just as it was harder and harder to conjure her parents' faces. They were standing on the other side of a foggy window. Ava could barely wipe the glass before it smoked over again.

"What sort of house was it?" Mrs. Anderson kept after her.

"The main house?" Ava asked.

"Never mind," Mrs. Anderson said. "Watch what you're doing, those stitches are crooked as a lightening bolt." Mrs. Anderson took up the rag she'd given Ava to practice on and tore out the stitches. "Pay attention this time."

Ava squeezed the needle between her thumb and forefinger.

"Feral as a squirrel, this one," Mrs. Anderson said to Mr. Anderson, when he came in, the cuffs of his overalls filled with frozen dirt.

"Got a start, at least," Mr. Anderson said. He cupped his hands together and blew into them.

Ava stubbed the needle against the table.

"Can't sew a stitch. That's what happens when you let a girl climb trees, wild as a circus monkey," Mrs. Anderson declared.

Mr. Anderson smiled at Ava and rolled his eyes. "Ground's hard as a rock."

The needle made small, satisfying punctures in the oilcloth, like peck marks left by a bird.

"Stop that!" Mrs. Anderson snatched the rag from Ava's hand, needle dangling from its white thread. Ava, surprised, knocked the matchbox of pins onto the floor. They scattered, a tinkling music. Ava started to sniffle.

"Don't move, I'll get the broom," Mrs. Anderson said. "It's nothing to cry over."

•

THE YOUNGER ANDERSON CHILDREN DELIGHTED in Ava's shadow puppetry. She transformed the thimble into a wash bucket, her index finger tripping over into it headfirst, stumbling in blind confusion with the thing stuck over its head.

"What's all this laughing?" Mrs. Anderson asked. Ava closed her hand around the thimble. "That's not a toy."

To Ava, the Anderson house itself felt like a puppet show. Eventually it would end and she would be allowed to trudge home, cheeks aching, lightheaded from molasses chews, craving a long cool drink of water.

•

AVA HELD HER BREATH, LISTENING to be sure Mrs. Anderson had really gone upstairs, then piled the torn trousers she was supposed to be mending on a chair, and slipped out the side door. She trudged up the rise toward where the men—Mr. Anderson, his grown son, and their hired man—were still digging the grave. They'd started out digging two side-by-side, but had given up and were excavating one wide enough to fit both coffins together. They had been digging for almost a week and the hole now swallowed them almost to the armpits. Their pickaxes thunked, February ground chipping off like slate. The men paused frequently to smoke or rest, hunched down on their hams, hot tendrils of steam rising from the exposed skin where their wrists stuck out between their gloves and the cuffs of their coats. The smell of the fire still lingered in the rattletrap branches of the trees, as though wisps of it had snagged there. Beyond the snow-swept fields, Ava could make out the husk of the house, windows gaping, a darkness that threatened to pull her in.

The men's voices traveled crisply over the frozen ground.

"Be a lot easier if we set one on top of the other," Mr. Anderson's hired man said.

"He'd be lucky, her under him for all eternity," Mr. Anderson's son said. He worked in town and came back only on weekends. The hired man slept on a cot. The kitchen table had to be moved out into the sitting room each night to make room for him.

"Who's to say it wouldn't be her on top?" the hired man said. "She rode bareback on more than just him, could tell by looking at her." And he and the grown son laughed.

"Shut your big trap," Mr. Anderson said. Ava's mother had been pretty.

Ava fingered the scab on her forearm through her sleeve, bumpy and raised, the shape of a cornflake. The whoosh of flames racing up the runner that lined the staircase crackled in her ears again, wild sprays of sparks as roof timbers buckled and crashed. Ava blinked hard, shook her head. She bent over and turned her face to the side, as though the memory were a pebble that might drop out of her ear. *Put it out of your mind now,* Mrs. Anderson said whenever she found Ava sniffling. *Put it out of your mind,* as if there were a drawer somewhere that Ava was supposed to shut it up in.

Raindrops splattered across Ava's sleeve. By the time she ran back down to the house, a gale whipped through the leafless trees, lashing the windowpanes. Soon the men were knocking their boots against the stoop, tracking mud across the kitchen.

"Looks like a good one," Mr. Anderson said.

"Make digging easier," the hired man said.

With everybody inside and the stove going, Mrs. Anderson had to open windows. Rain pelted the screens, spritzing Ava's face. Mrs. Anderson laid rags across the windowsills. Half Moon Creek, normally a dark trickle at the edge of the snowy fields, began to roil and brim. Veins of mudwater ran down the yard, joining larger streams cutting off into the ditch beside the road.

"A lot a trouble for a bunch a bones," Mr. Anderson's son said.

Mrs. Anderson hushed him. "It's the Lord's will."

"Setting a candle down too close to the curtain is what it is."

"That's enough," Mr. Anderson said gruffly. The brown finger marks where Mr. Anderson had hauled her up by one arm were faded to yellow. Ava had to look very close, to rest her chin on her arm, to even see them, though Mr. Anderson's singed eyebrows had not yet fully grown back and the burn on the back of his neck where the beam had fallen still festered, oozing a syrupy yellow discharge. He had carried Ava so far from the burning house she had started to feel the cold. She screamed and kicked. *Take me back. I want to go home.*

They sat down to eat. Mrs. Anderson served Ava a biscuit on her plate before the others reached for theirs. The children all drank from the same jam jar, but if Ava's lips touched it, Mrs. Anderson hurried to remove it, using her apron as a mitt. She was constantly wiping door handles and other places where Ava's bad luck might rub off.

Finally the rain let up. The hired man hauled the buckets up and set them at the edge of the grave and Mr. Anderson and his son carried them a short ways and flung brown leashes of water across the fence into the marsh Ava's father had once tilled. Mrs. Anderson insisted the grave water be thrown over the property line.

•

Ava hopped between frozen puddles—a satisfying *creee-ink*, like sheets of peanut brittle cracking underfoot. Mrs. Anderson talked with the ragman.

"Go say a prayer to your parents," Mrs. Anderson told her, fluttery and pink-cheeked. The ragman had paid her two dollars fifty for a basket of worn-out clothes and six pairs of home-knit socks. Mr. Anderson took Ava's hand, and together they walked up the hill.

The mound was large, as though a horse were buried there. Mr. Anderson dropped his chin to his chest, closed his eyes. He looked to Ava like a giant bat. There was no stone, only two wooden crosses. Ava tried to think of her parents and feel sad. Mrs. Anderson had packed her two thick wedges of molasses cake to take on the journey. The Anderson girls, in a fit of remorse, had each given her one of their hair ribbons.

Mr. Anderson straightened, blinking as though he'd woken from a nap. He reached for Ava's hand. His fingers were warm and rough with calluses, stiff like gloves even though his hands were bare.

"Ready, little dumpling?" the ragman, Erskine, asked. He lifted Ava up onto the wooden bench at the front of the wagon.

Mr. Anderson thrust his hands into his pockets. Mrs. Anderson waved frantically. By the time Ava twisted around to face frontwards again, she found they had already passed the charred shell of the rented house. She held the sack with the molasses cake on her lap. The horse's hooves clopped on the frozen road.

Erskine was lean and crinkle-eyed, his black hair and beard tinseled with silver. His head bobbed with the jolt of the horse.

"What's your name?" he asked.

"Ava."

"Your Christian name."

"Ava Pearl Mueller." Ava swung her legs and stole another glance at the heavy patchwork of flour sacks covering the bed of the wagon.

"What's under there?" she asked.

"Are we going to eat that cake or just smell it?"

Ava took off one mitten, wedged it under her leg, and slipped her hand down inside the sack. The cake was still warm. She held it out to him, but Erskine only jutted his chin at her. She ate both slices.

After a while, Erskine turned down a muddy track toward a sagging, unpainted house surrounded by fields. He lifted Ava down from her seat. Something that sounded like pebbles rattled in his pocket as he walked.

After Erskine pulled back the flour sacks and wiped the boards clean enough that she could read what was carved there, the woman who lived in the house was so overcome by sobbing that Erskine took Ava to the barn. She held her palms up to the nuzzling velvet noses of the horses. Cold wind whistled through the missing planks. The woman, done sobbing, fetched her coat, climbed up into the wagon and rode with them into town. A man helped Erskine carry the coffin through the iron gate of the hilltop cemetery and the woman pressed a small silver cross into Erskine's hand.

"May the Lord keep you," the woman said. When he tried to give it back, she squeezed his fingers around it until he cringed.

On the evening of the second day, Erskine nudged Ava awake. The white church steeple could be seen, surrounded by a small cluster of lights.

"Bellefonte, pearl of Spring Township. Now we have a little pearl of our own, don't we?" He winked, dug a hand in his coat pocket and held it out, gripping the reins in his other hand, watching the road. Ava looked down into his palm. A lemon drop sat beside a rotted tooth, encrusted with gold. The lemon drop was a cloudy yellow, but the tooth glinted in the weak light. Ava popped both in her mouth before he had time to realize his error. She kept the molar under her tongue the rest of the way, sweet metallic tang of lemon drop lingering in the slick crevices.

"Down we go, little pearl," Erskine said, setting Ava on the sidewalk in front of the white house. It stood very close to the street, no room in the yard for a climbing tree.

"Here she is, Fred," Erskine said to the woman who came out onto the porch. She was old and well-kept, though she looked nothing like Ava's mother, whose aunt she claimed to be.

"That man," she huffed, removing a hankie and shaking it out, as if to clear the air of Erskine. Ava would come to recognize this cross breathlessness in her aunt every time a man shortened her name, which she took as a kind of flirtation. On Erskine's tongue it was chaste and good-natured; he teased Aunt Fred as he might Ava, or any other child.

"I'm your Aunt Fredericka," the woman announced, as though it were an office to which she had been elected. "You're Millicent's girl."

Ava nodded, careful not to move the gold tooth around in her mouth, but Aunt Fredericka went on, as if she had not been soliciting any particular answer.

Aunt Fredericka sighed. "Well, your name is too short to be shortened. That's something to be grateful for." She went inside.

Ava spit the tooth into her palm and slipped it into her dress pocket.

"Come in, what are you waiting for?" Aunt Fredericka asked.

Ava tugged the screen door open.

Aunt Fredericka ushered her in, but did not wipe the door handle with her handkerchief, or the lip of the blue willow china cup Ava was given her tea in or the butter cookie she touched first, before choosing a larger, raisin-filled one instead.

"Look at those tiny fingers," Aunt Fredericka said. Ava slid her hands off the table and into her lap. "How would you like to learn to tat? Do you know what that is?"

Ava shook her head, wary of the coaxing voice.

"Here," Aunt Fredericka said, laying down a doily. "What does this look like?"

"A duck."

"A swan, isn't it? We wouldn't waste all this fine lace on a plain duck, would we? Now, let me see those fingers again."

Reluctantly, Ava slid her hands up and across the table. Aunt Fredericka covered her fingers with her own, closed her eyes, and breathed in.

"These hands. Oh what beautiful things will come from them," Aunt Fredericka said, opening one eye. Ava smiled, unsure of how the game was played, but liking Aunt Fred's flowery smell, the soft, powdery texture of her skin. "Yes. These hands are capable of many wonders."

•

WOOL COATS AND SHEEPSKIN EARFLAP caps parted. Ava walked through eddies of hot white breath, past hands dug into pockets, squeezing the warmth from baked potatoes that would cool and congeal by the midday dinner bell, curious stares, and up to the door of the schoolhouse.

"If she touches you, your parents will die," the girls hissed, braid-ends flicking like the forked tongues of snakes as they whipped their heads around from their benches to stare. Ava slipped her hand up her sleeve until she found the scar, probing its fleshy raised edge with her fingernail.

"What's on her head?" the boys whispered.

"A lice net."

"No such thing."

"Is so."

Ava's blond hair was poofed over her ears, braided, pinned in a roll at the back of her neck, and held in place by a snood, in the style Aunt Fredericka had worn as a girl. She drew her hand out from her sleeve, her fingertips smeared with blood.

The girls walked in front of her up the road after school let out, stealing glances behind them and whispering.

"Chase them," John Dougherty said, falling back with her. "They'll scream."

Ava looked at him, her hand up her sleeve, scratching. His hair was coal black and wavy and when he grinned she saw his front teeth were full-grown, giving him the friendly aspect of a rabbit. John Dougherty was nine, a year older than she, and had to be called by his full name to distinguish him from John Toomey and John Miller, until John-Dougherty sounded like one name.

"My sister will, definitely," he said. Myrtle Dougherty, Ava's deskmate, darted her pen into their shared ink pot furtively and sat with one leg overhanging the bench edge, ready to bolt if Ava tried to contaminate her. Erskine Dougherty was already a widower; she couldn't afford to take any chances.

"Try it," he encouraged.

Ava pulled her hand from her sleeve, leaving the newly formed scab intact.

John Dougherty took her slate and Ava stopped, waiting to see if he would stick out his tongue or fling the slate into the ditch, but he only stood there, waiting. Ava raced up the road, gravel crunching under her shoes, and the girls shrieked, scattering like a flock of startled birds. It filled Ava's chest with a swell of pounding, as though she had yelled as loud as she could and heard her own voice echoing all around.

This went on for some time. At the end of the school year, the children presented their gifts to Ms. Harty, who behind her back was referred to by a different, rhyming name. She was a chesty woman whose belly was swollen up, though she never produced any babies, only flatulence.

"You made this? How lovely," Ms. Harty said, examining the rabbit doily. Ava had sat in the light of the lamp for hours, learning to knot. A carbonated prickle of pride rose inside her. Ms. Harty raised the rabbit for the others to see.

A hush fell over the girls Ava's age, little gasps of admiration. Myrtle scooted in Ava's direction. The dark hair and eyes that on her brother were serious and watchful only made Myrtle Dougherty look sullen.

"Can you make a butterfly?" Myrtle whispered.

Ava nodded, biting her lip. Myrtle scooted closer, until their legs brushed. Ava sat taller.

•

AVA SQUIRMED, BUT MYRTLE HELD fast, hooking her by the elbow so that their hips bumped together as they walked.

"Maybe he'll ask you, before he goes," Myrtle said, tugging her arm.

"Why would he?" Ava shrugged free, her heart banging so hard that she held her books to her front, afraid Myrtle might see. Heat rose in her face.

Myrtle stopped walking.

"Maybe Clyde will ask you," Ava salvaged quickly. Myrtle considered this, turning it around in her mind, admiring the idea from different angles.

"He has to have a house first. I've always said I wouldn't marry a man who didn't have his own house," Myrtle said, taking up Ava's arm again. "And I have to have two good tablecloths," she hinted.

"I'll make you one," Ava said.

"Will you? I knew you would."

"Myrtle Dougherty is a dullard and a scavenger, like that whole family. I don't know what you see in her," Aunt Fred said when Ava came in.

Ava went to the kitchen, squeezed a lemon into the pitcher, filled it, stirred in sugar and skimmed the seeds off the surface. She set two glasses on a tray. More sweet than sour, it balanced out her aunt's mood.

•

AVA PULLED THE BAG OF regulation wool from her basket. Mrs. Harty was satisfied with Ava as long as she delivered the knitted socks to the Women's Society. Aunt Fred accepted, grudgingly, that Ava attend the Saturday evening meetings, not out of any special patriotism—knitting, even for a good cause, was a lowly undertaking compared to lace-making—but because it was necessary to keep up their standing in the community.

John Dougherty had wanted to take her to see the circus in Philadelphia before he left—he would join as soon as he graduated at the end of the term, but Aunt Fred had refused to allow it.

"If you let that boy ruin you, you'll regret it the rest of your life."

Ava packed up her knitting supplies.

"Put your slicker on," Aunt Fred said.

Ava sighed. "It's not raining."

"Is that what they teach in that high school, how to foresee the weather?"

Outside, the evening cool was just beginning to rise, a thick layer of warm air still hanging over the brick streets.

John Dougherty milled about at the end of Curtain Street, his hair slicked back with grease.

"Myrtle's going to marry Clyde Rasmussen," he said.

"Liar."

John Dougherty shrugged. "He came over from Zion last night to ask her."

They left enough space for a third person to walk between them, but as they left town and turned onto the Wingate Road, Ava let him drift closer. He shifted her knitting bag to his other arm and slipped his free hand around her waist, fingers playing up and down the whalebone rib of Aunt Fred's ancient corset, perfecting a tune only he could hear.

The old barn had blown over in a storm and was so overgrown with trout lilies it did really resemble a shipwreck. When he'd first taken her there at the beginning of spring, the checkered quilt had already been spread out, but now it was stuffed under a pile of boards, where the rain couldn't get at it. It smelled musty when they shook it out. She'd gotten used to the sight of his bare legs, which had seemed comical at first, hairy and very thin, as though they did not rightfully belong to him. She sat up. He lay with his head in her lap, batting at the half-knitted sock.

"Stop," she said. "I have to finish this."

John Dougherty collected her stray hairpins. "My toes will get frostbit and fall off."

"Who said they were for you?"

She took the pins back from him, holding the next in her teeth while fixing one in her hair.

"Let's go this way," he said, wading up through the tall grass.

"What for? It'll be dark soon."

The light was already fading, here and there a cricket. He tugged her across the creek, then dropped her hand, moving up the rise through thickets of scrub oak. Ava scrambled after him. He slipped over the ridge, as though Europe lay on the other side, leaving her behind. An indignant prickle rose in Ava. Already out of breath, she quickened her pace. She burst through the brush and he caught her hand.

"Down there," he whispered.

"The next time you—"

"Shhh!" John Dougherty hushed, extending an arm for Ava to follow his line of sight. "See it?"

"How can?" Ava trailed off.

"Must have escaped from the circus."

"What circus?"

"Shh."

Grazing in the clearing below, it caught a whiff of them and lifted its head. Ava drew in her breath, shrinking herself, making herself invisible. It regarded them, glass-eyed, then lowered its head. Its mane, striped as its zigzag coat, was stubby and stood straight up, electrified by the same current that needled up Ava's spine. Its white stripes glowed against black, like the skeleton of a horse.

John Dougherty squeezed her hand, pressed her palm to his lips.

•

THE FIRST WINTER, HIS LETTERS arrived every two weeks. Ava found them on the table, beside a cup of warm tea. The letters were always a little damp and wavy, but Aunt Fred asked so many pestering questions about what they contained it seemed unlikely that she had in fact steamed and read them. They were mostly frank and complaining and made Ava feel like a school friend, or a sister, as though he did not miss her particularly.

The meat's as tough as stewed shoes and the drinking water so grey you'd think the whole company had washed in it for a week.

Myrtle got letters too, though not as often. "Hear anything from John?" She would ask, twirling her hair and Ava would be forced to produce one, Myrtle's eyes flicking down, not really reading, looking for a word to jump out. "He writes the dullest things."

Still, reading into them, Ava sometimes thought she detected more.

The blisters are eating through my feet, but still I'm not tempted to sacrifice those socks. I keep them in my pocket. Can you believe, after all this, they still smell like trout lilies?

"I'd wash them," Myrtle said, flaring her nostrils. "That's the worst oniony smell. Oh, they'll say just any old thing in a letter, won't they? All Clyde ever writes about is his boots. They're torn or the hobnails pass the cold straight up like having two blocks of ice strapped to his feet. All he thinks about are those new Pershing boots; they haven't got them yet. The secret is to get them a size or two big and wear extra socks. Everybody knows that."

The day the news came, Ava sat at the table, re-reading John Dougherty's most recent letter, which had arrived that morning. Aunt Fred hovered at the stove, waiting for her to finish. She had taken an odd liking to him, now that he was safely removed from Bellefonte. The rapping was so frantic, Ava knew it had to be Myrtle. *Manners of a barn cat,* Aunt Fred mumbled, but stopped before she got to the doorway. Ava looked up. Erskine stood haggard, his face carved with lines. He had the telegraph with him.

There was no body. It took two months for the headstone to come from Philadelphia. It arrived on a Wednesday, the same day as his very last letter.

We're going to take the Chateau at Cornay. Don't let the name fool you. It's just a crummy-looking old house. The roof's still on it though, so if we don't burn it up too bad, it'll be nice to get in out of the weather for a night.
You know, I would chew off my own arm to get back to you.

It was only a fragment—no signature. Her name and address were not in his hand. A friend must have found it. It was strange to touch it to her nose, the same mildewed paper he might once have brought so close to his own face. If she closed her eyes, she could feel him separated only by this thin sheet.

•

AVA SAT AT THE WINDOW with her tatting board in her lap, tracing the loops and bridges. In the afternoons she watched kids trek home through the snow, younger siblings riding piggyback. Even after the snow melted, river churning with runoff, then lying still, sparkling with summer heat, Ava still felt the high water, her skirts soaked and heavy so that even crossing the kitchen was an act of tremendous will.

Bouquets of trout lilies turned brown on John Dougherty's grave. Widows called back and forth to each other, sweeping headstones—their names and dates of birth already inscribed beside their husbands'—but ignored Ava. Even the younger widows, girls Ava had been at school with, turned up their noses.

Ava took long walks, cutting through clearings, startling the white-tailed deer. They fixed her with wet eyes, as though they too thought they could make themselves invisible by standing still, then bounded off like stones skipped across the surface of a pond.

She avoided the shipwreck, where their younger selves lounged on the quilt. The world felt off-kilter. It was hard to know what was possible.

She hiked up the ridge, breath scraping the back of her throat. The clearing below was empty. The buzz of insects, then a sharp clap pulsed through the air.

She turned, trying to determine its origin, but it crashed in on her from every direction. She grabbed hold of a branch, wedged her toe into a crook and hauled herself up. She lugged and heaved until finally she could see out. Far below, a man waist-deep in summer grass was sorting the old barn boards. A white horse browsed nearby.

"John!" Ava yelled. The man looked up. A boy Ava hadn't noticed popped up from the grass, shading his eyes with both hands, which made Ava draw back. She waited until he turned, then climbed down gingerly, dropping the last few feet, knees bent, listening.

She skirted the clearing and came up around the other side of the horse. By the time Clayton Sinclair noticed her, she was picking flecks of black paint from its grown-out mane.

Little Harvey Sinclair stood up from the grey board he'd been kneeling on, wrenching out the rusty, square-headed nails and banging them straight before dropping them into a tin. He stared at her in a curious, friendly way. He was bare-chested under his overalls, little pink shoulders blistered. The clap of boards stopped. Clayton hitched one foot onto a stack of them. He was army age, broad and thick-limbed, but with his parents dead and Harvey in his charge, he wouldn't be going to war.

"We're going to built a brooder house." Harvey said. "The wood's still good. Good enough for chickens, right Clay?" he asked his brother.

Clayton Sinclair looked sun-drunk, like maybe he couldn't see any more than the outline of her.

"You don't think they'd care?" Clayton asked.

"Nobody to care," Ava said, though she felt a catch in her chest.

Clayton smiled, like she'd paid him a compliment. She held her palm under the horse's nose. It snuffled. Clayton shuttled boards to the wagon, and hitched it back up.

"Give you a ride back to town?" he asked.

Harvey sat between them, the three of them banging shoulders as the wagon rolled through the woods, nails jangling in the tin Harvey held in his lap. They stopped by the old farmhouse. Clayton washed in the yard, pumping water into the trough and splashing it up into his armpits and over the back of his neck. He went inside and came out in a clean shirt.

"That Sinclair boy's a workhorse," Aunt Fred said, when Ava came in. "The old man mortgaged that place up the yinyang, but he keeps going like he's going, he'll have himself dug out before too long. Anyway, farmers have a more natural view of things." Aunt Fred paused. Ava knew what that silence meant.

Don't care so much about a woman being intact.

Clayton Sinclair borrowed a car and took her to Milesburg, where some boards had been laid out in the middle of a cornfield. There were empty karo syrup cans with candles inside to keep the bugs down, ten cents a dance. Clayton Sinclair dug the dimes from his pocket. Ava tried to tell him she was sick of dancing, but he said he was going to tire her out. He must have spent two dollars on dances. He had a sharp, husky smell that Ava associated with men's bodies, though it was only the scent of shaving lotion. The lightness she felt had nothing to do with him. Just as his weight, her arm braced behind her head to keep it from knocking against the inside of the car door, his heaving and grunting were disconnected from the warm tide they gave way too. She cried, sobs loosing from their roosts, where they'd been hanging upside down in her ribcage.

"I'll marry you. I swear I will."

It was a relief, to be held.

•

"That old house is falling to the ground." Aunt Fred said, inspecting the table-cloths, wrapping up the blue willow dish set, her wedding gift to them.

It was Aunt Fred who took them to the Trust and Loan. Clayton hunched in a little wooden chair outside the banker's office, wearing the same suit he got married in, foot bouncing, until the paperwork was signed. They built a brick house with the money.

They were putting in linoleum. Clayton had gone into town for more glue and Ava was organizing linens in the stone-top dresser which was too wide to haul up the stairs and would remain permanently in the sitting room.

Clayton came home.

"Would you believe Gleason wants forty cents for a lousy can of glue? A couple old horse hooves, I could make the stuff." He shook his head and trudged up the stairwell. "Oh, and John Dougherty's back." His voice floated, disembodied.

"What?" Ava asked.

"Only got one arm left," Clayton called down. "Looks in bad shape."

Ava's chest tightened, as though she were holding her breath and trying to breathe at the same time.

Clayton crouched in the upstairs hall, painting glue in wide arcs. Ava stopped, both arms braced against the stairwell. "We can bring that bed up soon as the smell's gone," he said.

"John Dougherty's dead," Ava said.

"Army got their wires crossed I guess," Clayton said.

"What?" Ava choked. The baby, Russell William, stirred in his crib.

"Get on downstairs," Clayton said. "This stuff is pure poison."

•

AUNT FRED SIGHED. "HE'S REDUCED." She used the expression for any man who came back marked by the war, hobbling on a crutch or turning his head to expose the small, dark hole you had to lean close to and speak directly into.

Ava felt the heat of Clayton's upper arm through his sleeve, hat on one knee. She glanced behind her. John Dougherty sat stiffly, two pews back, his black hair unruly, as though he had walked to church through a blasting wind.

After the service, people filed past the pastor and backed up in a line to pay respects to John Dougherty. Clayton and Aunt Fred joined the line. Clayton held Ava's hand, though she'd fallen a half step behind him. She wore a pale blue dress with mother-of-pearl buttons, saddlebags of cooled sweat at the armpits. Under it, her chest was marked with hot red blotches. Erskine stood by, shaking hands, accepting congratulations. Ava extricated her hand from Clayton's. John Dougherty kept his eyes down, a tin-monkey shake. He had been right-handed.

That first afternoon, patches of milkweed lumped under the quilt, shadows of leaves tracking across their bare skin, bits of cottonwood fluff carrying on the breeze, Ava had told him. How, at first, looking up from her toy ponies, she'd been hypnotized the flame ruffling up the curtain, the heavy muslin disappearing in a wave of shimmering air, ashes floating on the warm updraft. It had seemed miraculous, like a tablecloth yanked off with the snap of a wrist, crockery and candlesticks undisturbed. It was only when the smoke turned grey and began to billow, filling the room, that Ava called out.

Standing before John Dougherty now, Ava wanted to seize him by the shoulders, to rattle him, to dislodge this memory and have it roll out into her cupped hands like a walnut, something she could close in her fist, contain, shield from the view of others.

•

CLAYTON HIRED THE LAUNDRYWOMAN'S DAUGHTER, Rosa, to look after the baby after Ava's disappointment. Bad luck, people said, though it hardly described the slick dark clot nesting in the cotton rag inside her bloomers. Ava stayed in town, where Aunt Fred could look after her. Clayton came to see her most evenings, his overalls streaked, standing so as not to dirty the edge of the bed, looking bashful and penitent. If she pretended to sleep, he stood self-consciously at the foot of the bed with his hat in his hands and his head down, praying, or sleeping, it was hard to tell. A few times, Rosa, a girl herself, brought the child.

On one of the last days Ava stayed in town, Aunt Fred went out. It was a weekday, still early. Ava walked along Curtin Street and up to the Union Cemetery, eyes on the path until she came to the low stone wall that separated the new annex, where John Dougherty's grave was. The stone had been hauled off, the empty box dug up. It was there that she met him, near the obelisk that marked the beginning of the war graves.

John Dougherty wore a wool coat, though it was too warm for it. His skin was sallow, eyes larger, darker, wilder. The empty sleeve swung as he walked, gravel crunching under their shoes. They followed the path back to where it entered the woods. There was a shed where the groundskeeper kept shovels, a push mower.

They walked silently. Their shoulders brushed once, turning a corner.

"You painted that horse," Ava said finally.

John Dougherty smiled.

"He shot it. It broke a fetlock, bone poked out just like a splinter. He said a lion must have spooked it, but I thought it was you. I mean, I thought it was your ghost, punishing me."

His fingers brushed her thumb.

"I cried all the tears in my body."

He caught hold of her fingers and held them, exploring the calluses where the constant friction of the tatting thread had thickened her skin, and pressed a small warm stone into her palm. She closed her fist around it.

"They call the creek that now, you know."

"Painted Horse Creek?"

Ava shook her head, flushing the way she always did when teased. "Idiot."

John Dougherty grinned, but he looked pained. "I may have done some things I'm not proud of. But that's not one of them."

"I thought you were dead." She wiped her eyes with the back of her hand. "Almost."

She sniffed. "We live out the Wingate Road. It's a brick house. It's not like town. It's so dark at night you can't see your hand in front of your—" she stopped.

John Dougherty smiled "I know what that's like."

"We planted apples. Bramleys, that's a pie apple. And McCoon's, that's an eating apple. Cortlands for cider."

His eyes softened. He looked for a moment like he would touch her face.

"I have a baby already," she said.

A tear ran down from one eye, but he did not lift his elbow to wipe it on his sleeve. He gripped her fist and held it to him.

"I can't," she said, pushing against his chest until he let go. She turned her head, embarrassed at how easy it was to outmatch him, without his second arm to insist.

"I thought you were dead."

"Would you rather I was?"

•

THEY WALKED DOWN THE PATH and out the main gate, Ava six paces ahead. To the neighborhood watchwomen polishing their windowpanes, it must have looked as if the two inhabited separate worlds—him a ghost of his former self, Ava Sinclair recovering from a disappointment—she's young enough, and one at home already, that's a consolation.

She followed Curtin Street, descending the steep dip. As children they'd tobogganed down in it, racing, hanging onto each other, shrieking until Aunt Fred called her home. How heavy-hearted she'd felt, leaving before the others. John Dougherty had stopped to watch her go, one arm behind his back, as though already practicing for when he would lose it.

It wasn't until she reached the bottom of the hill that she registered the pain in her fist. She had forgotten having given it to him. Sewn into the seam of his uniform, it had walked the streets of Europe, visited its cathedrals, its women—surely there had been women. Yet here it was, intact—gold and bone. It still held the warmth of John Dougherty's good hand.

MARC McKEE

You've Been Swallowed
by a Whale Only You Can Let Go

for Jamie Warren

It's no surprise that I hate it
when my friend is swallowed by a whale
even if it is only a dream of being swallowed
by a whale, the whale everything ever
all at once and thus a stupefying brick of cloud
borne by Manhattan's swaying pallbearers

as I think of how to try to bring her out,
and also thus whale after whale full of whales,
all the coffins, the urns, the urns' ins
and outs, the white whale
of the gone, the swallowed of all the nations, the ones
we feel sawed off from singularly, grief, grief

as ever a creature with an obscure orbit
and an appetite we are certain
in our treacherous, ordinary valleys
no light escapes nor can hope to contend with—but
this is why some days, in some instants,
in this instant, we must rise

and slip the cinematic tentacles
and slap the needle off the face of the beloved record
and charge into new dreams
like fools that won't quit singing.
The record spools and loops and pools
and floods into the air, the menacing atmosphere

a whale when a whale moves, an epic wave
taking forever to build
against what tiny forts we've made
from pillows and purloined fencing, our cups empty
and refilled a dozen times over, all our sheets in the wind,
our cultivated and distant loves, our locals,

our air. It's chased us so long
we think we're looking for it
until we turn into the dark and understand
we've been swallowed. It's always so easy to steer out
for those of them not in trouble.
But do they know there is a part of each dark

that doesn't go away and what to name it
is forever on the tip of our tongues
troubling the loose tooth of the heart?
The way you suffer the landscapes with your eyes,
here and then and next, arrives you in country of whales
not yourself a whale, but sympathetic. History blooms

and blooms through the blooms
its smoke and viscera, struck surely
and surely too seldom
with flashes of human kindness and sacrifice.
You don't have to kiss and apologize to that urn
every second, you don't have to shoulder history

every second, the shadow glides through Bloomington
as though on skates, it knifes down all the interstates
like a cloud of knives, the knife cloud a whale
but sing it up, sing it gone, sing light
and see it lift out of you
where it had been all this time.

Like the man sings, *If I see you struggle,*
I will not turn my back: sing that, sing it so aloft
it's a parade float: The Past,
hovering, real and powerful but not so mighty
it can keep you from the light waiting
even now for your next waking, sweet

as the sweetness of water is sweet
after a long walk out of the desert of the whale.
Even as I write this, the sun
converts long, sharp weapons into water
that the earth will take in
like your next deep breath.

MAGGIE QUEENEY

The Patient Part by Part

The patient has been left alone
but for his own body, strange
with taped tubes snaking
from the soft-blue veins, too long.

It has been too long since the patient
has seen his own naked knee.

His heart has turned into a tuber
bursting roots, binding his shoulders,
ribs, and back to the mattress.
The patient is turning strange.
The patient's body is turning

strange to the patient—a blanketed
mountain range, eroding riverbank
a nurse visits on the hour. Anonymous
as a temple's attendant, she reads
the temperature of the patient's flesh

and speaks to herself. The patient watches
the hate the attending hide as they stare
at their own hands moving, washing,
covering his body, part by part.
He watches as they bend to attend

as if in genuflection, faces turned
to floor, half-hidden, as if in pain.

MICHAEL VAN WALLEGHEN

Hand

In the powder-blue
snowflaked
            Heritage
Nursing Home lounge

all the wheelchairs
are watching
            URBAN
LEGENDS:
            PART TWO . . .

a holiday
            slasher flick
that even
            half-pajamaed

sleigh-ridden
            old St. Nick
is forced to watch—

surrounded
            by a sparkly
court
      of stuffed elves
and spastic reindeer . . .

until soon enough
                  blood
is sloshing everywhere

and a severed hand
all by itself
            crawls up
into my mother's lap.

Finely veined
                unwrinkled
and so far at least
                        barely
the slightest bit of blue.

It wants
            nonetheless
just to lie down now
and take a little nap . . .

But my mother
                    of course
wants it to play—

and so
        she slaps it hard
hard
        against her cheek

her heart
            the stupid arm
of her chair
                until finally

by suppertime
                    it's dead
for sure
            and every bit
as cold
            as zombie meatloaf—

and thus
            summarily buried
with some mashed potatoes
underneath her afghan.

Who needs it?
                    But little
little does she know

that tomorrow—
                    New Year's
Day in fact
            her vaguely
husband-looking
                    dim-wit son—

professor bullshit
                    baseball hat—
a scant
        elevator ride
too late—

will find it
            resting lightly
lightly on her throat
                    still warm

in his too late hands—
                    those long
small fingers
        still barely blue.

DEAN RADER

Self-Portrait: Postmortem

Imagine a poem that begins at the end, in that big boat beyond the end,
where things are both timeless and no longer part of time or even part of things,

which is a bit like picturing water without waves or light without the stars
but not at all like a sky comprised entirely of stars or the stars composed

of our thoughts about them, more like the body's bones minus their crushed music
or music free of meaning and misapprehension, but most of all like a sea

in which there is neither up nor down, forward or backward, depth or distance,
only the motion of stasis, the weight of weightlessness. There the poem bobs along,

lifting itself out of itself into the long lee of the hereafter, floating the way time floats,
like a leaf in a river made of leaves, no branches anywhere near or in the distance,

in fact no distance at all only infinite direction. And now picture the poet asleep in the boat;
you have set him there the way you might gently place a doll in a crib or a gun in the hand

of a man wearing a blindfold, and even now as you pull the trigger of his sail,
and propel him through the fast air of the unknown he is still here, which is to say,

nowhere, meaning, yes, we have now entered that space for which there are no words at all,
only the idea of words, a concept entirely impossible without the language to refute it.

Next, I will ask if you can imagine a reader sitting in a waiting room at a doctor's office,
a blur of magazines on the table to her right. She pulls a small book out of her bag

and opens it. Outside the building, a car stops or not at a crosswalk, a plane passes
in the sky above, or maybe it does not, a girl climbs to the top rung of the monkey bars

or perhaps she slips at the highest point and falls to the ground. Regardless, time is rolling
up its rope and heading to the shore, meaning the past hast done it again.

Lastly, imagine a poem that is not a poem at all but a kind of visit, a dream maybe,
in which you and I are talking, your face in my eyes, my voice in your head. You sit

beside me in the dark ride as the organ plays and our little boat lifts and drops over the edge.
We are so close, it is as if we have traveled the many distances solely for this. You ask if I hear

the violin, and I ask if you fear what awaits you. But you remind me that we
are not afraid of what we cannot see only of what we imagine.

Etiological Self-Portrait

Not with a bang but a baby's breath
not with a scream but a scratch,
not with the angel but its after-ash,
not the dead but with their dreams:

we begin to climb up into that which
we have only begun to understand—
time might be a cup of tea
or a hummingbird above the rose bush—

we never know for sure, just like now,
after a day of fog and heavy grey,
we wonder about the sun in its tiny wagon
of light and who might be pulling it.

JACQUES J. RANCOURT

Litany

One man every inch between bridge and canal
One man the antique plate blue ink a plougher ploughing a field
One man lost one man one man one man
One man died from one cure
One man the purple splotches the broken veins
One man the scarlet Karposi's sarcoma
One man all poppers and piss
One man the god of the sauna
One man the rabbit ears of a television set twitching
One man midnight's boxed glow
One man flickers one man static one man snow
One man slept with ten men and survived
Ten men slept with one man and died
One man the red sea splitting
One man the drunken dragonfly skimming the pavement
One man kept his secret a secret
One woman with a husband with a fever
One hundred men then one hundred more
One man the school bus without a driver
One man the suspension cables without a bridge

CATHY LINH CHE

The opposite of the ocean is no ocean.

These days, I fall asleep
to the sound of my own
reading.

I haven't ridden
a roller coaster
since my 20s.

I held a fistful
of coins then.

Numbered them,
but really they
were uncountable.

Yesterday, I wrote
a love song.
The radio dressed up

and called into a field—

That echo of dreaming—
Once, a man smiled at me
with all his teeth.

Then the field was lavender
and the wind braided
into my hair.

I am sitting in the kitchen
without socks, just skin
against linoleum.

Last year, we went
to New Orleans.
It was Valentine's day

and we ate King's Cake,
excavated a baby
from its sweet sticky flesh.

I kissed your cheek.

We ate gulf shrimp
at a round table
at the back of a smoky bar.

We were so full in those days.
Then I reached into the hearth
and pulled out the kindling.

You sustained me
with the warmth
of that low fire.

How does it feel to sleep alone?

One sock by the bed,
one on your foot.

You were
the foothold
that offered

itself up.
I'm not crying,
but, oh, I cannot stop.

RACHEL RICHARDSON

Theory of Desire: The Animal

*The lobster doesn't like it
when we eat him*, my daughter posits—
a point I knew was coming
after naming *chicken* in the neighbor's coop and *chicken*
on her plate. *Animals eat other animals*, I shrug.
This is hours after I've read
that Captain Pollard's crew, 74 days adrift, drew lots
to choose who would sustain the others
with his meat.

I want a claw, she says, reaching.
Behind the breathy traffic
on Water Street, we hear a shout
rise from the bar, a staticky cheer
that resettles as the crowd resumes drinking
and another player on the wide screen
saunters up to bat. *The animal that gets eaten
never likes it*, I say, though
I read many men, perhaps even
Pollard himself, lay down in the bottom
of the whaleboat, covered themselves
in salt-crusted canvas, and prayed.

*I like my lot
as well as any other*, said Owen Coffin
before his childhood playmate took up the gun.

Inside the claw, the sweet flesh.
Inside the bones,
even of a starved man, the marrow.
The blue whale's skeleton, displayed

in New Bedford since 1998,
still oozes rich oil onto the museum's wood floors.
It is fragrant and golden in hue.

Translation Folio

HAYDAR ERGÜLEN

"pulling the sea back and forth with longing" especially on the foggy nights Istanbul has in winter when the ferry lines are shut down. There's more to it than just geography, of course. Ergülen has lived a long time in Cihangir—the neighborhood of artists, actors, intellectuals—and, during their courtship, his wife lived many years in Üsküdar—conservative, Islamic, a gateway opening to Anatolia.

In both of these poems I've made several compromises. Rather than tease out all nuances of each pun and allusion, I've simply chosen whatever seemed the most interesting. I've also tried to keep to about twenty lines in length while also trying to make sure the lines in English match the Turkish. (Although I've made alterations when that results in an awkward line-break in English.) I'm reluctant to translate meaning-for-meaning if it means losing the form. At the same time I resist translations that rewrite in order to preserve rigid form. My strategy is to keep the meaning as close to the original as I can and then add elements of the form back in. The form of these poems is loose at the level of the line but replete with rhetorical shifts. I've sought to avail myself of the same resources in English, even when they don't match up exactly. Thus while I might not choose the exact element Ergülen chooses or I might leave out this one or that one, we're drawing from the same pool of structure and sound.

Ergülen's work makes full use of the techniques developed by the Second New poets, a generation before him. This means the minimal punctuation and the flexible syntax of Turkish verse work together to create multiple possible readings across lines. Where the English veers too closely to obscurity I've opted for clarity even at the loss of a potential reading. I've also opted to work punctuation back in, hoping that the remaining imagery retains something of strangeness and ambiguity in the original.

When I approach a poem like "Rose Breath"—heavy with word-play, grammatical repetition, and lexical ambiguity—I look to sound as much as language. While "nefes" simply means "breath," it can also imply "soul" or "spirit." But in the case of "Rose Breath" it means something more. Ergülen is Alevi, a sect with what might be called an Anatolian understanding of Islam. Alevi worship incorporates wine, dance, and songs called *nefes*, so perhaps "hymn" would be an apt understanding. These songs draw on a long history of folk poetry and they form the initial section of Ergülen's most formally complicated book, *Üzgün Kediler Gazeli*. I decided the rhythm was more fundamental than the rhyme—that it allowed the images to jump more freely—and I hope that its song-like nature is apparent also to the English ear. It's also worth noting that the capitalized letters seem to have a secret, mysterious meaning—they form no acronym in the original. Instead, they set up the sonics of the phrases which follow. My solution was to translate the following phrases as sonically as possible and then change to capitalized letter to suit.

Blue

You were wearing nothing but the rain.
For my meaning it's enough that you were naked.
How was it that your eyes reminded me of how
a poem has to be written? I believed in you like this:
I write poems in order to believe, whatever your eyes
remind me of, that is what I believe in, your eyes
remind me of Cihangir—from an Üsküdar
so impoverished in memory, I dreamed this: You
were blue, pulling the sea back and forth with longing.
Softly gently, for the sake of beauty, I believed
in the rain, the rain we owed so much to, I believed
in a cloud in a far-off blue girl's eyes, I believed
that it would pour down rain within us, that even
if you'd had a blue raincoat you'd have been soaked.
I believed in your body like this, luculent,
reminding me of what a poem needs to be written:
You were so naked nothing was left in you but poetry.
I believed in what your body was reminding me of.
Even if they don't remember me, I know
that sometimes those far away don't wait for letters

and some poems too can't wait for the rain to stop.

Rose Breath

the letters my mother swims in are the sea
if B goes Beşiktaş-ward, E passes Eminönü
on each and every ferry   her alphabets
have passed her youth by like silent ships

the ghazal my mother voyages in is her home
R is the rose's name, M the mottled merriment
in each bashful moment   her footprints
have carried the silence of the rose hours

the love my mother divines within her is in the deep
if L is longing, W is a whimsical garden
which gladdens every love   her eyes
have hidden the lost elegance of mercy

for sure my mother's retired her allegiances
if only she'd been coy to a C   if only
my soul didn't have to disembark so soon
she'd be a ferry transporting a rose

Fog

There are two cites of the night, one fuming
in my eye, the other like rain steaming
in a falling mist. Why have you left behind
this sleepless city for me? You're in all cities
instead of the one I wouldn't dare to be in.
It's not night you want but instead to plunge
into the city's long dark gaze. I understand
your eyes, they've never yet plunged against
the eyes of anyone who's able to forgive.
It's not only when we hold off from one another
but also when we dare to draw near that hurts
our eyes—and only eye can forgive eye.
When my eyes hurt this much, who can forgive them?
Not mist, not insomnia—my eyes separate,
fail to close together, like two cities, remote:
One still sleepless as if eye to eye with all of us,
the other in the mist, open as eyelashes.
Who would have broken this silence? I cannot
see even a single word in your loquacious eyes.
Our eyes don't touch each other in the two cites of the night

and if no one's eyes touch anyone's, what's the point of poetry?

Translated from the Turkish by Derick Mattern

FEATURE

Three Essays on Contemporary Publishing

JOHN O'BRIEN

19 Things: more thoughts on the future of fiction

(Note: O'Brien's essay, "31 Questions and Statements about the Future of Literary Publishing, Bookstores, Writers, Readers, and Other Matters" appeared in the *Review of Contemporary Fiction* in 1996. This piece is an extension of that original essay.)

WHEN I FIRST WROTE MY essay on the future of fiction about twenty-five years ago, I had much to say on several topics. In re-reading that essay that appeared in the Review of Contemporary Fiction, *an issue co-edited by myself and a newly arrived faculty member, David Foster Wallace, I was surprised by the accuracy of the predictions. But now in old age, one does not worry, or even think about, the future: the future belongs to others to worry about and to speculate on. And so I have far less to say, just a few odd-and-ends comments that may be more about the present than the future.*

1

LET'S START WITH AMAZON. AT the time of my first essay, Amazon was cause for laughter: who would buy books without being able to browse? But Amazon has succeeded, though at the expense of a number of independent and chain bookstores across America. Driving other stores out of business was not an unfortunate byproduct of the service and discounts Amazon offers, but part of a business plan to take over bookselling in America and become the near sole source for books. And Amazon has now set its eyes on publishing. Will it succeed? Quite possibly, or at least cause enough damage that only very small publishers doing books out of their basements and garages with little overhead will be left; even these will barely survive because the means for distribution will be Amazon.

And now that Amazon—depending upon what it needs to be on any particular day—is a distributor, a bookstore, and a publisher, both a producer and supplier, competing on terms that no one else can match: Which is why of course the United States has anti-trust laws, none of which seem to apply to Amazon. One wonders why Amazon hasn't completed the circle and bought or merged with Barnes & Noble, even if the ultimate plan would be to close down the retail stores and do all business on-line.

It's still too early to tell whether Amazon, in building its empire, should have become a publisher before wrapping up the supply-side by consuming Barnes & Noble. Rather than starting its own publishing arms, it could have then consumed Random Viking. And since the Obama administration has apparently suspended all anti-trust laws for Amazon's sake, what would stop this lock-step method of controlling books in America and beyond?

2

AT THE SAME TIME, AMAZON has also become a philanthropist to various literary organizations and publishers, thus effectively silencing them concerning the intentions and practices of this Goliath. PEN, for instance, should be very concerned about "free speech" when a corporation such as Amazon threatens to control what's published and what's made available in the marketplace of ideas and expression. Others that pride themselves on being watchdogs of publishing and book-reviewing remain silent as they benefit from Amazon's largesse. Their moral indignation, which characterizes much of what they have to say, bypasses Amazon's door. Can the do-gooders be bought off at such cheap a price?

3

FUNDING FOR LITERARY TRANSLATORS HAS increased in recent years, as well as it should. Ignored in all of the attention paid both to translators and never-ceasing conferences and roundtable discussion concerning translations are those who take all of the financial risk and make the final decisions about whether translations will make their way into the world: the publishers. Translators have fought hard for their rights and increased compensation, but publishers as a group have not, perhaps because there are so few of them who are even interested.

4

THE INTENSITY AND FREQUENCY OF discussions about translations have lead to a false assumption that the number of translations has appreciably increased over the past five to ten years. I will here just point to numbers that concern adult fiction and poetry published in the United States and (selectively) in the UK. The best guess is that there has been a modest increase of perhaps 30-40 titles, and this increase occurs amid the reality that the total number wavers between 300 and 400. Quite typically one finds some very brave but very small publishers pushing the numbers upward, though these presses are usually publishing as few as two to ten translations per year and can hardly be thought to be making much of an impact despite the impression that some few of them make that they are fighting a Holy War (and perhaps they are, but with a slingshot). My point here is that publishers are usually not asked to sit on panels, nor asked the inevitable question: "What would cause you to publish more translations?"

5

IF PHILANTHROPY AND GOVERNMENT IN the United States do not see the value of bringing the literary art of other cultures into the English-speaking world, then how do small presses carry the burden? Let MacArthur, PEW, Ford, Mellon, and Rockefeller assume responsibility. The last time I meet with Rockefeller, at the request of the head of the translation program of Arts Council England who had come to the States to try to form a worldwide coalition of funders for translations, Rockefeller began the meeting by saying, "I have no idea why I agreed to this meeting." Welcome to America!

6

UNIVERSITIES AND NONPROFIT LITERARY PUBLISHERS would seem to have much to offer each other. But . . . Robert Creeley said to me one night as Dalkey was about to move to a university: "Get everything you can going in because once you're there, all that they will do is take away." Strangely, some years later, I saw him again at a dinner party the night before meeting administrators at another university to discuss Dalkey Archive moving to their campus. He pulled me aside and said, "I hear you're meeting with the provost tomorrow. If they ask you to tell them how they will benefit from bringing Dalkey here, walk out." The next day, that is exactly what the provost asked me. The provost was one of those awful creatures whose ambition was to keep moving up the administrative ladder, from one school to another, inflicting damage at one place, using that damage to sell themselves on the basis of how deeply they cut expenses at the previous school while initiating four new campus-wide physical fitness programs.

7

ACADEMICS ARE THE LAZIEST PEOPLE in the world. And they dress badly.

8

MY ADVICE TO YOUNG PEOPLE: I have none. I once did, but no more. The older you get, the less you know. Plato was right.

9

AMERICAN PUBLISHING IS ON THE verge of collapse. It's based on an economic model that cannot sustain itself.

10

THE LITERARY PRESSES IN MINNEAPOLIS HAVE always had a different model for surviving, central to which are the foundations in Minneapolis that created and sustain a literary scene there by funding literary presses, and, as a consequence, causing presses to relocate there. This model of financing could have existed in other American cities, but the foundations said no. On a few occasions, I made my best effort to persuade the MacArthur Foundation to support literary presses—and not just Dalkey—to create a scene that could cause magazines and presses to stay in Chicago or to move there. MacArthur said no. One year, the head of culture, after I described what had happened in Minneapolis, suggested that I move Dalkey Archive there. There was the opportunity to begin something in Chicago, and the head of culture at MacArthur suggested that Dalkey leave Chicago for Minneapolis. I said that Dalkey had started in Chicago, that it was my hometown, that I wanted this for Chicago, and that MacArthur should move to Minneapolis.

11

THE UNITES STATES IS A third-world country in relation to supporting its literature and bringing literature to the United States. Some of the smallest countries in Europe, and some of the poorest, spend more money to support their literary culture than does the United States.

12

COMMERCIAL PUBLISHING IS DOOMED—AND that leaves the small presses, forever on the verge of going out of business. But the very small presses, those doing fewer than 10 books per year, have a chance to survive because they have one or two or no paid employees. They do short print runs, and don't have the money to properly support their books. And yet this lack of money is also what makes the model work financially: their problems begin when they have enough money to hire a third person (the other two are founders). But will these presses survive their founders? Most likely not.

13

AGAIN: WHO HAS CONSISTENTLY BEEN left out of the discussions concerning translations? Editors and publishers: which would seem to be an odd omission. These two figures—oftentimes one and the same person—are the ones who put up all or most of the money. Editors tend to be perceived as people who have an "opinion" (not to be taken too seriously) about such matters as word choice, syntax, and readability. Oftentimes, the office of a Ministry of Culture or a book office will reserve the right to approve the translation, or even to appoint the translator, after which the translator has the right to accept or reject an editor's "suggestions." And the publisher? The publisher is hardly thought of at all once the decision has been made to have a book translated and published. And if a translator is late in submitting the translation and the deadline is past for when the book had to be issued according to the funding agreement . . . well, in that case, the publisher must then absorb the full cost of the translation. And all of this is quite the opposite for a book written in the "home language." The publisher and editor make a final decision as to whether a book is in acceptable form, whether changes need to be made, and whether to proceed with publication: this power is granted to the publisher because it is the publisher who must make the decision to have the company's name on the book's spine and take the financial risks. PEN has taken the lead in creating discord between translators and publishers.

14

HOW IS IT THAT EDITORS and publishers do not at least have a place at the table or on the panel when funders call for a meeting to address issues of translation? In all the years that I have been publishing translations, there has been only one meeting to which I was invited to tell a funder what the problems were in doing translations, and what would cause both myself and other publishers to increase the number of translations. Once!

15

WHAT I THINK MOST ABOUT these days is who will become the next generation of Dalkey when I am gone. If Dalkey came into existence to publishing books that would stay in print regardless of sales and be the protector of those books (now over 750 in print), who will protect the protector? The United States does not have a record of success in keeping a publishing house intact after the founder is gone. The names may continue, but not the values. Of the nonprofit publishers, Graywolf, Copper Canyon, Milkweed and BOA have successfully gone into a second generation. These are not encouraging statistics: four out of so many.

In brief, I've no idea what Dalkey's future will be.

16

THE NATIONAL ENDOWMENT FOR THE Arts is responsible for the existence of many small presses in the United States. Had literature not been included as a fundable art form in the 1960s, many small presses would not have survived those difficult early years. The founders had no experience either in publishing or running a nonprofit organization. They had a vision of change, and here was government money to support what they did, as long as the "organization" (these were not organizations) would be nonprofit. Graywolf, Coffee House, and Milkweed were among the first on the scene. When the Mellon Foundation in 1990 or thereabout became interested in funding nonprofit literary presses, they could find only nine that fit the minimal criteria of: (1) nonprofit status, and (2) a budget of at least $100,000. Dalkey had just reached $100,000 in grants and sales.

Move this up nearly twenty-five years, and these presses have become much larger, while two have ceased to exist. Leaving aside the Minneapolis presses with foundations there providing on-going support, the others still hang on a shoestring. And yet, regardless of their status as "organizations" even to this day, they exercise an impact on literature in this country far beyond their organizational capacities.

Back in the early nineties, even many of them would describe their roles as being "farm teams" that found and cultivated young talent that would then move on to commercial houses. Though I objected to this description and thought the opposite (that the commercial houses found the authors, paid them fairly well, and then would dump them when they weren't making enough money), we certainly could not compete with the large publishers in the marketplace. The situation has now changed: these presses, and many others like them, are responsible for almost all the poetry that's published in the United States and much of the non-mainstream fiction, and of course about 98% of the translations. And yet almost all of these presses are endangered species. Who in American philanthropy is thinking in terms of how these presses will survive and become permanent and continue into the future?

I can imagine that the National Endowment would not welcoming the following suggestion—but who else is there on a national scale to undertake this as an issue?—but here it is: there should be a fund, a sustainability fund, that provides multi-year operational grants for these presses, ones that have survived, let's say, twenty or more years, have produced a certain number of literary books, and now have overhead expenses they could not have imagined twenty or thirty years ago: insurance and retirement plans for employees; warehousing; audits; professional bookkeeper; rented space; updated equipment; a human resource manager; business plans, office managers: need I go on? All of those expenses that have nothing to do with the core mission but eat away at the money intended for that mission.

And let us say that right now in America there are about 10-15 presses that fit this profile.

17

AT ONE POINT, ALL ROADS seemed as though they would lead to Minneapolis. A scene was being crated there, in large part because Minneapolis foundations were funding nonprofit literary publishing, and nothing like this existed in the United States. Publishing in the United States was being defined by two cities: New York and Minneapolis. In fact, Dalkey Archive came very close to relocating there. Brining in a few more presses and literary magazines from other parts of the country would have made Minneapolis the city to be in, and the city to go to. But something stopped this migration, and I have yet to figure out what this is.

18

THE TIME HAS COME TO wrap things up. Dalkey Archive is on the verge of seeing whether there is life beyond its founder. Which reminds me: Douglas Messerli of Sun and Moon Press (now renamed as Green Integer) and I used to have arguments when visiting Minneapolis for meetings with the Mellon Foundation (a New York foundation that held its meetings in Minneapolis!). Douglas would argue that a press had its "moment," that after a while it starts to parody itself, and should end when the founder does; I'd argue the opposite, that there was no good reason to have spent 30-40 years creating and running a press, only to have it end, something akin to constructing a building with a plan to tear it down in 30 years (this, in fact, is Chicago's general building plan). We've yet to see who was right, and perhaps we will end up in the same place regardless of the difference in our views.

19

AFTER ONE ATTEMPT TO EXIT this random serious of observations, it is indeed time to turn off the lights. There will be no further updates.

JESSA CRISPIN

The Self-Hating Book Critic

REMEMBER WHEN EVERYONE WAS SUPER upset about newspapers cutting their book review sections? People picketed. People with better things to do and ideas in their heads stood outside of newspaper offices and held up signs and said words through bullhorns and performed other related physical activities. Until, I'm guessing, their feet got tired and they all shrugged and went to Starbucks.

Most of these people's employment was in some way tied up in the newspaper book review section. Either they were writers worried about their next books not being covered and thereby boosting sales, or they were critics themselves, worried about their paychecks. I point this out to illustrate that there was no big public outcry that book review sections were being cut. A few readers may have written a letter here or there, or strayed into the picket line until their feet also got tired. But as a whole, the cutting of book review sections was met by the general public with a shrug.

This all happened several years ago. More and more book sections collapsed, more and more longtime critics were laid off. And still, no one outside of those inside of the business of reviewing books quite noticed.

•

IT FEELS STUPID TO TALK about the crisis of book criticism when the entire industry is in crisis. We have no bookstores now—now that Borders bullied so many independent shops out of business and then died itself, now that Barnes & Noble is in death throes, now that Amazon rules publishing and treats it like a British landowner in 19th century Ireland.

"Oh, you're starving to death? That's too bad, it's your own fault really. It's a shame you can't have any of that nice food you've been growing, because you know that's ours now. Because we said so. If you could go outside to die, that would be helpful, it makes such a mess when you go, you know."

Then there's the no-one-reads-anymore hysteria, the lack of supportive careers for apprenticing writers, the MFA deathtrap, etc. It feels self-indulgent as a critic to say, "But the whole critical structure has broken down, let's talk about that." The critic only comes into play when the books are actually produced and put onto the market, meaning their jobs are tied into this whole decaying, rotting mess of an industry. Which is why it's amazing that the only thing book critics really got exercised about was the cutting of newspaper review sections, not any of the rest of it. Surely there was another point where they could have placed their picket lines to do some good.

•

AND LET'S LOOK, FOR A moment, at what the death of the newspaper review actually meant, because that keeps getting lost in the nostalgic haze of men who remember a simpler time, when literary culture was tied intimately into popular culture and authors could still be rock stars without writing about magicians or vampires or whatever. The death of the newspaper review meant the end of the literary authority who would declare that books by straight, white men are always the best of books. That books by the conglomerate publishing houses are the best of books. That literary culture exists only in New York City. That literary critical culture is a lofty, apolitical space of objective assessment. That is essentially what the critical culture told us for the fifty years of the post-war literature (the peak for literary rock stars like Mailer, Updike, Nabokov, et al.) and its seemingly never-ending influence.

Actually, there are some newspaper book review sections still in existence for some reason, but now the rowdy online culture regularly keeps tabs on them. They count up the number of books written by women and people of color and LGBT writers that are reviewed by the newspapers. Or the number of women, people of color, and LGBT reviewers who are hired to write the reviews. It is always a small fraction of the whole. And that is what all those people on the picket line fought to save: a sexist, racist, elitist system.

Some people still confuse the newspaper literary culture—a small subgroup, almost a fetish really—with literary culture as a whole. Mostly those people are the people the newspaper literary culture is both serving and comprised of, those silly people in the picket lines. White, straight, male New York writers and critics.

I can't imagine why that might be.

•

BUT ALSO ALARMING IS THE number of women, people of color, LGBTQ, radicals and weirdos, all the wonderful et ceteras of the world, banging on the doors of the *New York Times* to be let in. As if inclusion will give them legitimacy. As if there isn't a fucking cover fee. As if that fee weren't parts of your human body.

I want to tell them: this world is not for you, you are better without it. Outside the gates, not in. This world was in fact, in part, designed specifically to keep you out. It does not want you. It will not nourish you.

And just because you gain entry for one fleeting moment, do not think for a second that you haven't stomped all over the even less desirables on your way in, don't think the system has suddenly become tolerant.

But people outside the city's walls long for entry; it is the set-up. That is how the city controls the frontier.

More interesting would be to exist outside the walls, and learn how to raid the city for whatever it is you need.

•

JUST TO BE CLEAR, THE Internet is not the frontier in this particular metaphor. Some of it might qualify, but most of it is just suburbs. The most respected, the most quoted and blurbed from, the most prominent and respectable of the literary critical apparatuses online are run by white men. They write about books published by conglomerate publishers. They pretend literary culture exists solely in New York, although MFA programs will also get attention. Other than a few eye-rolls about Amazon hijinks, they too are apolitical.

The city sends the suburbs their goods, the suburbs are grateful. The suburbs praise the city, the city in turn nurtures and feeds the suburbs with advertising dollars, book advances, and entry visas.

People like to think they live on the frontier, that they are pushing boundaries and living rebelliously. Nobody *really* wants to be James Joyce, though. When it comes down to it. Totally inaccessible and publishing poison, forced to self-publish with the help of two (inadequately celebrated) lesbians, thought to be a madman, and still cursed to this day. No one really wants to be James Joyce, living in borderline poverty with an insane daughter and a layabout son, quietly changing the world but very rarely, if at all, acknowledged for it. So completely out on the frontier his books were confiscated and destroyed by multiple governments.

But everyone wants to think they're James Joyce, in their cozy teaching jobs, in mortgaged homes, writing about the same things that everyone else is writing about. They want to think themselves renegades but they still want to be regularly petted by the authority. They look at their surroundings, and they think, *I can see grass, I can see sky, this must be the frontier.*

It's not. Check your paystubs, it's not.

•

FOR A CRITICAL CULTURE TO be vital, it has to be aware of its placement in the system. It has to see that system as broken. It has to respond to its brokenness.

It makes sense to me that when the system goes wobbly, the critical culture responds by saying, "From now on, we will only run positive reviews." It is a long list of publications and critics who have come out saying this, from *The Believer* to *Buzzfeed* to assorted Internet communities.

But that of course is not criticism, it is enthusiasm. And enthusiasm only happens in long form when all uncertainties and unknowns have been weeded out. When expectations are met.

It is a way to regain control. Uncertainty causes anxiety, and when things are already uncertain due to a literary system in flux, it is easier to close off, to shut the gates, to only admit those whose entrance is guaranteed. To, you know, review your friends.

Anxiety's primary function is to ready the body for action and for change. It is a complicated uprooting process, the gathering together of energy and focus so that when you decide what to do, you are able to do it. But only reviewing positively, closing off the doors of each individual subculture, creating communities of enthusiasm—that is not making a decision. That is the opposite of it. You are shutting all the windows and doors and trapping your anxiety in there. Smiles become forced and plastic-y, and the anxiety becomes, *Do I really belong here? Do they want me here? How can I ensure my placement here?*

•

GIVE A PERSON ABSOLUTE FREEDOM and probably what they will do is just copy the person closest to them. The anxiety of making a decision under absolute freedom is too much to bear. There is surely only one way to do things right, and all of these other ways to do things wrong. It's why the Internet culture is just a copy of newspaper culture, but with a few *fucks* and *shits* thrown in.

The removal of the newspaper book review and the rise of the Internet literary culture gave us all absolute freedom. So we all just basically recreated newspaper culture, because it was easy to replicate and had worked for them for so long. Surely it was the right thing to do.

•

IT'S HARD TO SAY WHAT value the literary critic provides to the larger culture. And I say this as someone who has spent the last twelve years of her life engaged in this activity. Don't think there weren't nights where I woke up with the thought "My entire purpose in life is to help people make decisions about which books to buy; I am simply part of someone's marketing strategy," chilling me to the bone.

There's the value that the literary critic can provide, but it is so often buried under needs of that critic to tend to one's career, to boost friends' books, and that burning desire to make one's opinion heard. That value is, thinking a thought out loud, following it through centuries of other people's thoughts, synthesizing it with your own thoughts and experiences. Books are vehicles for ideas, but ideas have no purpose until they are forced into contact with minds and bodies and experiences. Critics can put ideas into action, through the juxtaposition of idea and world.

And books are deeply personal things. Wept over, treasured, passed along. Not external objects, their function is to become internal. Sometimes the fit needs adjusting, that is another thing that the literary critic can provide.

Literary critics have value. And yet sitting here I cannot come up with a single name of a critic who has played some sort of role in my life. Elizabeth Hardwick? But really only for her fiction, her essays never did that much for me. Jenny Diski? But really only her personal essays. I am struggling here. And yet surely there have been some.

Maybe it doesn't matter that I can't remember a name. There were books that got into my hands thanks to critics, and there were books I was able to think my way through thanks to some assistance. It is probably right that they disappeared in that act, their identities dissolving so that the author could take their place. One should probably distrust someone who tries to make their name as a critic, someone whose goal is to be known for performing this act.

I am trying to remember what dragged me into this role to begin with. Books had served me, I wanted to serve them back. It must have been as simple as that.

•

IF ALL WE ARE DOING as book critics is propping up those in power, the conglomerate publishers and the unthinkingly celebrated, we are failing at our jobs.

If all we are doing as book critics is pretending there is such a thing as objective assessment of literature, we are failing at our jobs.

If all we are doing as book critics is assisting people in making a choice as a consumer, we are failing at our jobs.

If all we are doing as book critics is looking at the book and not the system that it came out of, we are failing at our jobs.

•

I AM A SELF-HATING BOOK critic who is failing at her job, daily. But the act of failing, and trying to understand that failure, is an interesting one to me. So I will keep at it, never quite getting it right.

JANE FRIEDMAN

The Future Value of a Literary Publisher

Since the late 1990s, I have been educating writers about the publishing industry. For the first ten years, most conversations centered on how to write better, find an agent, and get a book published (and then another). The big question on every writer's mind was: Do I have what it takes? And I would retort with: Do you have grit? Because dogged persistence was the biggest commonality I saw among successful writers, at least those who could be said to make a "living" at it.

By 2008, the weight of the conversation had shifted to print versus digital challenges. Many of us, both inside and outside the industry, have become consumed by the question of how long print will last, how much we have to compromise our writing and editing time to cultivate an online presence, and if it's the "most exciting time" to be in publishing or actually the worst.

We've all been in that conversation where we've made a proclamation about whether we favor print or digital, and when we favor it, and why we favor it. We muse on the difference in hand feel, smell, navigational memory, marginalia, and attention. And all of these things are intertwined with childhood associations, emotional milestones, and matters of personal identity.

But this talk is ultimately a distraction from the real challenges faced both by writers and publications—and especially by literary publishing. The problem is not whether print will survive, but how literary publishing adapts to a world where to publish something has lost value. As Clay Shirky writes, in *Here Comes Everybody*:

> In a world where publishing is effortless, the decision to publish something isn't terribly momentous. Just as movable type raised the value of being able to read and write even as it destroyed the scribal tradition, globally free publishing is making public speech and action more valuable, even as its absolute abundance diminishes the specialness of professional publishing. For a generation that is growing up without the scarcity that made publishing such a serious-minded pursuit, the written word has no special value in and of itself. . . . If everyone can do something, it is no longer rare enough to pay for, even if it is vital.

At a 2014 AWP panel,[1] Morgan Entrekin, president and publisher of Grove/Atlantic, identified two primary challenges facing literary publishing going forward: distribution and discoverability. But these challenges are not unique to literary publishing—they affect every single producer of media, large and small, and they've been long-term, persistent challenges. Furthermore, distribution is only a future challenge insofar as literary publishing is focused on print retail and bricks-and-mortar bookstores. Access to online distribution is now available to every author, business, and publishing company. *This* is what increases discoverability complications. The self-service, plug-n-play tools to publish *and* distribute have created not just a crowded marketplace, but a decreased value on the function and process of publishing. This has become a dilemma for commercial publishers in particular, who face increased competition from self-publishing authors, digital presses, and Amazon's own publishing program.[2] Hachette, one of the Big Five, was even compelled to leak a document in 2011 explaining why publishers are relevant. Could such a thing even have been fathomable twenty years ago?

To be fair, Entrekin's comments focused on how publishing needs *diversity* in distribution channels. Opportunities for books to get discovered by readers are disappearing and becoming limited to a few big companies, such as Amazon, Apple, and Google. It's largely Silicon Valley companies and the tech industry that drive what the future of book distribution and discoverability look like. A 2012 Bowker report revealed that where readers purchase books has dramatically shifted. In 2010, about 25 percent of books, whether print or digital, were purchased through online channels (that means Amazon, mostly). By the end of 2012, that percentage was closer to 44 percent. Most industry experts estimate we're now at 50 percent.

One of a publisher's primary strengths has been getting an author's books distributed to every bookstore or appropriate retail channel. As bookstores and physical retail become less and less important to book sales—and to an author's discoverability—what purpose does a publisher serve?

For literary publishing in particular, the imprimatur of a house remains important. It's not enough to simply publish; literary authors must be published by a certain *someone* to achieve the "right" types of reviews, coverage, awards, and attention. Literary authors are also concerned with quality editorial relationships that can nurture and support their careers for the long term, which presumably a literary publisher cares

1. 2014 Association of Writers & Writing Programs Conference, "The Business of Literary Publishing in the 21st Century."

2. For five years straight, Harlequin has reported declining revenues despite being one of the strongest commercial publishing brands in North America. Reasons for the decline include increased competition from independent authors, extremely competitive pricing, and decreased physical bookshelf space, among other factors.

about too, and is more able to offer, as opposed to a commercial house, which is less likely to be patient in the pursuit of profits.

In this way, an independent, literary press is often in a better position than conglomerate-driven publishing. They can more readily play the long game, be happier with small or "quiet" books, and focus on cultivating what I'll argue is imperative in the Internet era: community. But doing that effectively means that editors and authors have to give up some long-held beliefs and myths about online marketing and what it means to develop . . . dare I say the dirty word? . . . *a brand*.

·

In 2011, THE EDITORS OF *Triple Canopy* wrote a long essay on publishing in the digital age, "The Binder and the Server."[3] They spend a great deal of time explaining their efforts to design their online publication in such a way as to "slow down the Internet" and allow readers to focus. This will become important later on; for now, I want to bring forward a facet of their discussion, where they explain why their publication doesn't allow comments:

> Even after our redesign, which further facilitated our connectivity to social-networking sites, there is no way to "talk back." Everything published is carefully edited, often elaborately produced, and properly attributed. As far as the website is concerned, Triple Canopy has only authors, no friends. . . . If online publishing is to distinguish itself from the rest of the Internet's information stream, it mustn't settle for the easy terms of online friendship. It needs to maintain a degree of idiosyncrasy and difficulty.

Plainly illustrated, there you have the biggest threat to literary authors, editors, publishers, and supporters: outright hostility toward readers and discouragement of community. This position is *not* unique to *Triple Canopy*; it is commonplace in literary publishing. Regardless of what philosophical line of reasoning might justify it, the result remains the same: stand-offishness and the overriding attitude that engagement or interaction is a suspicious activity. The primary focus should be on the art; the rest is base. It is distraction.

Yet, by the end of their essay, *Triple Canopy* discusses their additional focus on readers:

---

3. *Art Journal* 70, no. 4 (winter 2011): 40-57, http://artjournal.collegeart.org/?p=2644.

. . . we have begun to address a third constituency, our readers, in a manner that we hope changes how they conceive of their relationship to *Triple Canopy*. Our readers have provided much in the way of moral support, but little of the material variety; for the sake of *Triple Canopy*'s long-term sustainability, we believe some percentage of our public need to think of themselves as subscribers. ... We're hopeful for the subscription model, if not necessarily optimistic. As a first attempt at attracting broad support, we recently organized a Kickstarter campaign. . . . We were heartened that 338 individuals pitched in, and grateful for the thirty-five thousand dollars raised.

Triple Canopy could rightly point out that not settling for the easy terms of online friendship has not apparently hurt their cause, though I have to wonder how much more support they would have garnered if they didn't seek to build difficulty into the experience of their publication. Regardless—and maybe surprising themselves at what they've built—*Triple Canopy* succeeded in building a community that has translated into sustainability for their publication. My theory is that they offer something essential that everyone seeks, online or off: *meaning*. It's not so important what *Triple Canopy* offers, but *why* they offer it. Whether I agree with their philosophy or attitude or not, they've attracted a following—online friends!—who believe in their mission and why they do what they do. Further, the people they attract have something in common with each other, which is the start of a community. *Triple Canopy* could take that same mission and produce a Tumblr, a newsletter, an annual event, an intellectuals-only café in Brooklyn, a line of clever stuffed animals, and serve that community through a variety of mediums and channels. People don't care as much about the *what* as much as the *why*, and this is the hope and strength of literary publishing.[4] (Notice this has nothing to do with print versus digital; each is simply a substrate through which to serve a readership.)

This is where conversations about brand have to start, and why brand doesn't have to be a dirty word. Brand should evoke an immediate and clear response that's not about sales, marketing, or promotion. The brand should evoke and emphasize the *why*—what the publication or publisher stands for. This takes time and is not an overnight process, and it's partly built on what *other* people say about you or what they value you for.

Perhaps the most important reason why this has become so critical—putting aside the fact we now live in a time where no one need struggle to find something quality to read, *even if we limited ourselves to reading only that which is free*—is disaggregation.

---

4. Here I must credit the ideas and talks of Simon Sinek, author of *Start With Why*.

Being able to cherry pick an essay from *ABC Review*, a poem from *DEF Review*, then a short story from *GHI Review*, and consume it seamlessly and distraction-free in a longform-reading environment such as Pocket, leads to three industry-changing behaviors: (1) readers have less reason to consume a publication in its entirety if they're not 100% committed to its reason for being (the *why*), (2) readers are less committed to any single publication if it doesn't interest them from cover to cover, and (3) a publication's design and reading environment, or an issue's larger context, becomes meaningless. This brings us back to *Triple Canopy*'s essay that focused on its extensive efforts to "slow down" the Internet reading experience. Today, it is largely irrelevant how a site presents content, because avid readers will increasingly import content into their preferred reading environment, usually when they are prepared to "lean back" into reading, a phrase coined by *The Economist* to signify that moment when we focus attention on reading (as opposed to "leaning forward" as part of a multi-tasking work environment).

While disaggregation has a more powerful and immediate effect on literary journals, magazines, and online publications, book publishers face the challenge too; the proliferation of endless (and quality) digital content that we can save and read for later can take us away from the to-be-read pile on the nightstand or what's hidden behind our reading app icon. One can easily fill all available reading time by simply keeping up with a self-curated list of articles saved to Pocket, scrolling through friends' links from Facebook or Twitter, or opening up Candy Crush. The less visible and immediate physical books are in our lives (because bookstores disappear, because books become digital, because of the competition from other media), the more important it becomes for every publisher to think beyond the next book on the release schedule, and consider how to engage their community in a variety of mediums and channels. The words on a screen or a page may remain central, but they become one expression of the brand, not the *only* expression.

In an essay that remains as relevant (and unheeded) as the day it was published, "Context, Not Container"[5] by Brian O'Leary offers one of the secrets to any type of successful publishing of the future: we have to stop being so attached to our containers, and think more about how we're relevant to our reading community, who now turn first to digital tools for discovery, information, and entertainment.

•

IN CLAY CHRISTENSEN'S NOW CLASSIC business text, *The Innovator's Dilemma*, he describes how low-quality upstarts in any industry are, at various stages, ignored, ridiculed,

---

5. *Book: A Futurist's Manifesto*, edited by Hugh McGuire and Brian O'Leary, http://book.pressbooks.com/chapter/context-not-container-brian-oleary

feared, and eventually (when it's too late) imitated. The legacy players within an industry are rarely able to innovate in the same manner as a new entrant, and the new entrants ultimately disrupt the traditional business and enter the high-quality range of the market. In print journalism, we've already seen this disruption at work with the rise of news sites like Huffington Post and the decline of newspapers and periodicals such as *Newsweek* and *Time*.

We can either ignore or ridicule Buzzfeed, Upworthy, and similar sites for their low quality, or for headlines such as "It's Often a Controversial Issue, But One Stunningly Illustrated Picture Book Handles It With Grace." Or we can take a page from their book, because they've got at least one thing right: Most of us want to read, watch, or feel something that has meaning and potential to provoke a life change, or help us see the world anew. If faced with a choice between reading "A Mind-Blowing Short Story That Changes How You View Love," and the Spring 2014 issue of *ABC University Literary Journal*, what would you choose? Chances are you're going with the experience that has offered you some context, unless you're already a devoted community member of *ABC University Literary Journal*. And therein lies my point.

Without a framework and context for what is published, literary publications can feel virtually indistinguishable from one another. Journals especially are guilty of making work available but not known. One might say there's a good excuse for the failing: literary publishing's mission or calling usually relates to producing art, not marketable commodities. But then this mission or calling needs to be defined and marketed to a target reader community that is engaged and committed to the survival of that mission.

The good news is that the digital era has dramatically fragmented the audience for media: we don't have to consume only what is best marketed and advertised. We each have more tools than ever to find exactly the right book, magazine, or experience that fits our mood, interest, or aspirations. The algorithm, silently at work behind millions of online transactions, is getting more and more powerful at identifying what each of us wants to see next, and this is an opportunity for every publisher. You can identify and directly reach your potential audience, without needing special distribution, without needing a large advertising budget, and without having a print book. But doing this requires what is often missing from the equation: the brand that knows what it's about and can convey that to an intended market. It takes time to build a brand and audience, and develop a real, valuable connection with readers, and it's a very different game than the one that is (and will be) played by the Big Five in New York. As Richard Nash once theorized at his own website:

> Basically, the best-selling five hundred books each year will likely
> be published like Little, Brown publishes James Patterson, on a TV

production model; or like Scholastic did Harry Potter and Double-day Dan Brown, on a big Hollywood blockbuster model.

The rest will be published by niche social publishing communities.

Literary publishers produce niche work, and are poised to become leaders of the community of readers *and writers* who have matching missions and belief systems. Literary publishers can add value and credibility to niche communities, through the act of publishing of course, but also through other forms of leadership and support that go beyond print and extend into events, services, grants, fellowships, reading groups, etc. Building community is primarily about intimate knowledge of and respect for a community, combined with creativity and imagination in serving it. Publishers that survive, whether they focus on traditional publications or digital media, must become indispensable to the communities they serve. While at one time a publisher might have been indispensable by communicating quality ideas and stories by remarkable authors, a publisher who does that today—and nothing more—can be seen as merely adding to the burden we all now face. There are too many wonderful things to read, and too few sign posts as to what's worth our time. Thus, the literary publisher needs to be a beacon, to offer a strong signal amidst all the noise, and organize ideas, content, and stories within an identifiable and useful context. Otherwise, many of us will turn away because we simply can't find the time to understand or discover the meaning or the quality of what's presented to us.

CHARLIE BONDHUS

streetwise

the houses on whispering rod lane are nicer than the houses on lantern lit lane, though not as nice as the houses on matroyshka ave or even the ones on rustling sedge road or paper pipe trail, though definitely nicer than the ones on bean street and a ton nicer than the ones on old musket road which is close to cabbage street and everyone knows the kids on cabbage street are not ones to fuck with anymore than you'd fuck with a kid who lives on or even near war path cuz even the dumb kids on tadpole turnpike know not to fuck with the kids on war path even if they've never been past shady trails, hell, even if they've never even been past pussy willow pike, whose kids everyone fucks with, even the kids on kangaroo court, because they know that the kids on pussy willow pike have money and money makes you soft which is why i built my house on sand when the property on rock was so much more secure, cuz i couldn't let people think that i had money to live on rock because then they'd think i was soft and i just couldn't have that and besides the houses on sand are almost as nice as the houses on rock though neither's quite as nice as the houses on water but still you can't have everything and it's better for people to think you're not as nice than to let them think you're soft.

Turbine room—Power station

What was there to do but gawk at the wheel and the wheel within the wheel? The turbine never moved, and a family of jackdaws had built a nest in the rotors. When we were first brought to that room they flew into a gap in the wall. The turbine was still, even when we slept, though we had dreams about the sound of moving metal. We stood in front of the gap and felt cool air. We said *it must lead outside*, but it was too narrow for us to follow. We took turns sticking our faces in as far as we could. In our dreams, turbines ground bone and feather into meat, which we ate. What we longed for more than anything was movement. When the jackdaws returned, one was carrying a small yellow flower; another carried a snarl of twine; the third had a mangled piece of cloth. When we first arrived we slid our hands along the walls, so cold they felt wet. We speculated about the gap. The only sounds we ever heard were our own voices and the jackdaws' gripes; there was nothing else except for the dead turbine. The first jackdaw dropped his flower. The second one carefully placed his twine in the nest. The third jackdaw released the cloth, which fluttered before landing near our feet, and we realized it was actually a piece of paper on which someone had written a word, either *wheel* or *whirl*, not that it mattered.

WESLEY ROTHMAN

Whiteness

This blizzard swarms as time

swarms, stings, crowds us

relentlessly, all deepfreeze and wind.

Flakes, weightless bone shards,

attack from the flanks. From every sky

a blitzkrieg of little devils,

their wily antics, their grave

burrowing beyond skin and calcium

to what must be our ghost

intangible in the marrow. This white,

not the invisible freeze. Not

sacrificial pilots. Neither the intangible

undermining nor a coat of frozen

throwing stars, melded ice locking

        us in place. What swarms and stings

camouflages with blizzard. It works

        from far off, commanding wind

and chill and fluid word;

        it works from within

like time, beneath the skin,

        in every bone, ungraspable

in there.

CHRISTOPHER BRUNT

404 PAGE NOT FOUND

Behind the internet we can see / is another internet, / a truer one. It eats / our wartime secrets, it records / the permutations of our slow-decaying / faces all day, each / & every night.

There was a writer who wrote / the Novel of Novels before / his hideous death. / That book was never found. / I will not tell you, "This book / is every book, re-coded into one." / "To be known in perfect / understanding" is what it feels like / to read this book, so the story goes. / Some people, internet people, / believe the writer did not die, / he's secretly alive, still writing. / To raise himself again when we need him most. / Others have proof he was murdered / by the local government. / All of these people are important / fools. Zealots for the talmud of a dream.

Tonight I get offline / and walk the country, / looking in at every glowing-white face. / And who / these days, is anything else? / What with the air tasting like human chalk? / What with fear in every sinew of the radio wave. / Even the rats are hung up / on old ghost tales, / whispering in our walls about the great snake king / who sheds his mystic skin each night. / The instructions of their ancestors / coded upon his scales. /

BERNARD FARAI MATAMBO

You Don't Want the Light
to Find Out What You've Done

You, me and Martin Luther King Jr. being black together. We are on a highway, somewhere where the ears of corn are low. As if the Indian bones in these hills had something to say. You tell me it's Nebraska. That corn looks Nebraskan is your excuse. The way my girl could be Persian when the weather permits.

We have given speeches for free before, but not since Iowa. Iowa has been our dessert. We are off west now on the gravy train, our lungs beating virginal across the open states. Where did they lynch men like me for gazing too long at white women?

In Illinois they hung two men by the Blue Front. And not until 1942 was a man tried for holding another man captive. For labor. That was the nearly true end of slavery. But still I am waiting for a morsel of good faith at the courts of public opinion on the redemption of Iron Mike Tyson. Waiting for my fist to clear the foggy eye of God. The way v.d. shots calm down the particulars, keep the herpes away, watching by the rubble.

I used to think these tollgates here were border posts up in arms, uniting the states. And this country was one huge jukebox. It explained the slotting in of coins, quarters tumbling down in a jig, sly. Money is deep as skin, knows no enemies like water. Watch it love you a lungful, coming through.

Somewhere near here a young man was killed, picked in a bar and nailed to a fence. Beat all night like a tattered flag, kept the crows away. He too remained resolute on the stakes of the law.

I was not one among that number who called the king wacko, but in that matter too I harbor my shame. Once in a while I doubted his marbles. What with blanket, what with all that and the other; coming through.

I am still wondering about being black enough. The way light sisters wonder if sunscreen remains appropriate for black girls in summer.

And if at all collard greens remain self-affirming.

I am in want of my egg over easy, my sunny-side up. I am still searching for a room dark enough to hang my skin in, keep it calm, let the light come in.

In the Throat of the Heavens' Guide

And should the revolution take place between your thighs, brother leader, blame hallucinogenics; it is only the mothers of the brave who weep, and my blood is weak with forgetting; how it trembles.

They will peel him out of a hole like Hussein. Or a mansion in Abbotabad. There is air and non-air. My friend tells me the colonel prefers tents, and face cream, things with meaning.

Perhaps they will find him in a French boutique in Tunis, lip-sticked and getting his hair done like the sisters up in Harlem, air-conditioning across summer.

Still, mother, I do not believe in the music of oceans; too many of my bones want to return home. The beating of my blood, Angola.

And should the revolution take place between your thighs, brother leader, pick the itch: there is no honor in clenched teeth. There is air and non-air.

My friend tells me that after the urethra's slow hymn and the gunmetal blues of other genitalia eventually the syphilis climbs upriver to claim the mind. Still there is no truer love.

And should the revolution take place between your thighs, brother leader, execute a strategic retreat. What saves us but the wind through the eye. Burn Al Aziziya, burn.

He will be in his desert library taking a nap in a womb chair between Nietzsche and Gogol. There is air and non-air.

My friend tells me he has a sweet tooth for agbada and Gabbana. They will find him in a mall flowing in the rivers of his robes. He will want penicillin and a pack of Doritos.

Still I often wonder about Sani Abacha, the Viagra, and whether the Indian women knew of Mobutu and the hemorrhoid; the scent of hours the sheik burnt watching himself, pitch-perfecting.

Always I am a slave—half-ape, half-child. What saves us but the wind through the eye. Born of the gun, Mother. Give me sight, so I too may see. An eye for an eye, our scrambled world.

Catechism

April 1994

You must have known better. Twelve years old and you were in the perfect blur of the world, the nuns like ants crawling everywhere, worried sick out of their habits and pantyhose. Particularly Sister Catherine.

Sister Catherine & her breasts, the daft youth in her knowing eye, & how the catechism class numbers kept climbing up over them, as though they were the very fountains of youth lit with the very song from the Pied Piper of Hamelin's wet dream, the one in which the children return to him, their nimble mothers in tow.

Because who didn't want to be saved by her, be confirmed in the flesh of her low hips, learn how to receive the body of Christ with a throbbing jaw, an anarchy of gears shifting between your thighs as her lower lip curled, pleading for the mercy of her open tongue saying, The Body of Christ; the Body of Christ, Amen.

Because that must have been when I like Saul saw the light of my bearings and yet was left longing for it to cut me through to blindness. My eyes shied away, the quiet limbs on the convent's screen washing in the foam of the stream. The thwarted hack of an axe through brawn, a brow wet with the effort. & then they were coming, bodies tumbling down the stream like manna from heaven.

Remind me again, dear love, of that time when the world was as young as we were and I was lit white with urges, light as the shroud Christ yielded when he gave up his tomb, sick of sleeping alone and dreading the eternity of it, when he sought himself some company. Of this earth no poetry shall come; of this earth no poem. Amen.

ROB STEPHENS

Kyrie Eleison

in the Anathema of Night

for I am the bleeding eczema on Your arms, the off-pitch
    cockroach mumbling like crinkled paper, an ingrown
hair You should have plucked, for when You say sheep I shit,
    when You say obey I oboe, when You say made from clay
I sputter and burn and dig farther into Your chin, Lord, I drink
    Kool-Aid from Your wine stems and swallow Your gum,

for I am mostly water and a multitude of bacteria gnawing
    the flesh of my intestines, I am hardly a shed of blood
or a quark of earth, I am a half-house for molecules, a periodic
    table of decadence, a frog pickled in the formaldehyde
of fickle, a tape deck of insolence losing my magnetism,

for one morning I leech-loitered behind the levee and hacked
    the head of a moccasin striking my boot and drank
dark rum and stood in swamp so the murk rose to my waist,
    I felt the envelope of earth and kissed the snake,
let the voodoo juice swash my temper and listened to drone
    of drunkenness, I sang the praisesong of the Mississippi
and clutched a handful of weeds and thought I might drown
    on the nectar of solitude, I might wither and melt
and bloom into a venom to be consumed by the next vagabond,

for nights I tremor at the thought of being zapped
    like the dead filament of a bulb, electrons erased
like the locust that flies to the light, the grayish haze of arson
    over my eyes with no angel no demon no purgatory,
blotted-out me at absolute zero, absence, dearth, the cut

wick of candle burnt to core, the vibrations
of the saxophone settled into line, static and sonic shock
    when organs shut down and night shuts down
and the brain stem powers off but there is no plug to pull,
    just a notion that my genes will be the marrow
of my ancestor's success, that I will be and am dust,

for You are the mace-hammer, the icy hot healer-human,
    the euchre chrism of black and white, the baptism
of candlelight rainbow, the high notes swelling to orgasm
    in the flying buttress cathedral, the swarming blackbird
army formation fluttering like wind chimes but attacking
    like a geyser, the dirt and tarballs and drainage
of the city flooding the drywall, leaving mold apocalypse,
    You are the filth that I will become, the ash,
and yes, Lord have mercy as I brackish Your soup.

LYNDA SEXSON

The End of Wheat

THE WIND WHIPS FROM SANCTUARY to sovereignty, slapping a weathered paper against his shin. In one light he might be taken for a bronze-greaved Achaean, but in another, a man up to his knees in debris.

He peels off the litter, letter, leaf, or leaflet.

Grandfathers, four and more grandfathers ago, had pulled back the skin of the prairie and patched it up with wheat and corn.

The grandfathers had read a pamphlet promising *Rainfall Follows the Plow.* They said that men who had gone for gold shouldn't have to go without cornmeal. They hoped to trade up barrels of flour for the good life for their sons, and even for their daughters.

Sons, descending by sons of sons, cut up and sell off scraps of land. Double-wides and split-levels encroach upon amber fields and umber hills. One-room startups with twice-over additions crouch under the Tobacco Roots, bluer than the sky.

Flags wave over each domain, like tiny, belligerent nations staking out broken trikes, battered campers, dead refrigerators and reliable generators.

He goes inside, tossing the old paper onto the kitchen table.

A spider is in the sink again. She picks up the paper, urges the striped-legged spider onto the vanishing writing, and carries it outside. He follows her saying, "Spiders don't really come up out of the drain; they fall from the ceiling." The boy watches the spider skitter under the pickup. The paper blows against the step. She picks it up like a point in their quarrel.

His motorcycle waits for him to change the oil and unclog the witches hat. They haven't ridden together, carving up canyons, eating up highways, since the boy.

"It isn't leaking," he had said, when his bike stained her mother's patio. "It's marking its spot." She had not laughed. But pressed against him and the wind, she hadn't cared that they had one helmet between them or that his words were on loan.

They had gone all the way to Kansas to a motel full of bikers gathering for a pheasant hunt. He called it their honeymoon. She stayed in the room while he shot at birds. A sign was posted in the bathroom: *Please Use Gray Towel for Gun Grease and Blood.* He took her home and she didn't even think about leaving until after the boy was born.

He says again, "Rednecks get new fridges like everybody else; they just keep the old one in the yard for parts." She never laughs.

The old barn has become an automotive mausoleum. *Sapphire Flour* fades on one side and *Freedom Is Not Free* is freshly painted on the other.

The wind twists and snaps the flag, looking like a bloodied runaway trying to escape across the roof.

She drops the old paper back onto the table, as good as a goodbye note. She takes the boy to her mother.

He waters the geraniums sweetly planted in the tractor tire. If she returns, "She'll see red flowers first thing."

A. G. PERRY

Little Fox Woman: Translation and Erotic Text

Language is not everything. It is only a vital clue
to where the self loses its boundaries.
—Gayatri Chakravorty Spivak

La femme au petit renard[1]

The Woman to the Little Fox
The Little Fox Woman
Small Fox Woman
Little Fox Woman
Small Foxy Woman
The Little Fox's Woman

•

What am I doing? I do not know. Violette Leduc, I apologize. The French inside me is adolescent, learned mostly in high school. Everything is a direct equivalent. This = that. Even attempting to translate your book's title transforms me into the young woman waiting outside a Paris patisserie the morning after her arrival, trying to figure out how to order a sandwich because j'ai faim. I have hunger. I am hungry. J'avais faim.

(I was hungry at the time and it was an ongoing state of hunger—at the time.)

•

Vingt-quatre, vingt-cinq, vingt-six, vingt-sept, vingt-huit, vingt-neuf, trente, trente et un, trente-deux, trente-trois, trente-quatre, trente-cinq, trente-six. . . le fracas. La table remua, les grains tombèrent dans sa jupe.

Elle ne s'habituait pas à l'envahiseur. Il la secouait toutes les cinq minutes aux heures creuses, toutes les deux minutes aux heures de pointe. Le revoir, l'attendre, le suivre,

---

1. Violette Leduc, *La femme au petit renard.* (France: Éditions Gallimard, 1965).

l'apprendre, le retenir, se familiariser avec le cataclysme, se presser d'arriver au ter-
minus avec lui. Elle sortait, la méthode s'ouvrait, dictait. Atteindre d'abord la guérite
de la vendeuse de billets de loterie, flairer dans une entaille le relent de la malchance,
stationer à côté de la grotte du marchand de journaux, se presenter à l'escalier du
métro Jaurès après avoir traversé à trois heures de l' après-midi le passage clouté du
boulevard de la Villette.[2]

•

I = je
would like = voudrais
(voudrais is more polite than "want")
a = un
(un, not une, because what I want is masculine)
sandwich = sandwich

•

I recognize three words
I can translate into
my first language: woman—
little—fox.
What they mean
together, I do not know—
yet.

•

To translate is to be involved in a love triangle, to submit to a "three-part structure"
of desire.[3] The three sides of the love triangle are the translator, the departing text
and its author, and the arriving text the translator creates. Language, communication,
approximation, effort, culture—all of these create a ripe environment for seduction
and frustration.

---

2. Ibid. 9-10.

3. Anne Carson, *Eros the Bittersweet.* (Champaign: Dalkey Archive Press, 1998), 16.

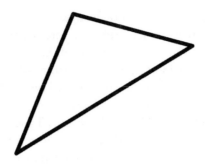

Speaking of the figures in Sappho's fragment 31, Anne Carson writes, "It is not a poem about the three of them as individuals, but about the geometrical figure formed by their perception of one another, and the gaps in that perception."[4]

To translate well, I have to admit that I cannot always see the object of my desire. To translate at all, I have to admit that sometimes I want the text to do what I want it to. I cannot see or understand all of the words I search for.

Translators take the risk of being bad lovers.

•

I could not have found myself on a map. I walked from the hostel where I and the other new au pairs were staying, following straight lines, remembering street corners, so that I could find my way back in time for the afternoon meeting.

On a bench in a park across from the patisserie, I waited, staring at a window decorated with breads and pastries too elaborate, too beautiful to eat. A mustard-colored awning shaded the window. Gold lettering said *Patisserie*. People went in empty handed and walked out ripping apart baguettes, croissants, brioches, taking bites.

Mumbling to myself, "Je veux. Je voudrais. Voudrais. Voudrais," I was auditioning verbs.

•

Van cadre, van sank, van cease . . .

---

4. Ibid. 13.

Homophonic translation can get me into trouble, can get me into a group of activists in sinking vans that quit running.

Say I hear a language I cannot (yet) speak. I try to make sense of it, listen for cognates, for tone, and context. Where is the meaning? Is he/she asking for directions or making a joke? One bottle a pop. Two bottles a pop. Why do I need an equivalent? Because it will make me feel better, make me feel as if I have four hooves on the ground and can finally start running?

•

Twenty-four, twenty-five (*I forgot twenty-five the first time through*), twenty-six, twenty-seven, twenty-eight, twenty-nine, thirty, thirty-one, thirty-two, thirty-three, thirty-four, thirty-five, thirty-six. . . the ~~fracas~~ (*uproar?*). The table ~~remua~~ (*overturned?*), the seeds (*grains?*) fell in her (*I assume a woman. technically, this could be a man*) dress. (*actually, remember "robe" is dress. "jupe" is a skirt. how wonderfully subversive if a man. could that kind of delicious ambiguity occur—extend—in English?*) fell in her skirt.

•

Before I was born, I began to inherit language. Language became part of my body before my body touched air.

I impose myself on languages I do not know well, natively, or at all. The moment a rush of wordsound comes toward me—through the atmosphere or the page or signs—and bounces off my ears and skin, I get out the bridles.

Involved, implicated, my body has a sense, before I even think, of what sounds right. I imitate those sounds, approximate them, and Stalling is right: "The inadequate attempt to sound out beyond the comfort of one's primary language brings readers to the edges of their inherited language bodies, but also makes the membrane more porous at the same time."[5]

•

---

5. Laura Mueller and Jonathan Stalling, "Phonotaxis: The Way We Travel Through Each Other," *The Conversant*, 10 Dec 2014, theconversant.org/?p=5231.

She (*gig is up now, girl!*) was not habituated to l'envahiseur (*hate? but that is sound logic, logic according to sound. la haine—envahi—hate? no idea. maybe invade?*). It was shaking her every five minutes ~~aux heures~~ ~~creuses~~ (*on the odd hours?*), every two minutes ~~aux heures de pointe~~ (*on the even hours?*). The to see again (*to see him or something masculine (a noun) again*), to wait for him (*yes, because these are infinitive verbs, not nouns*), to follow him, to (*understand, but that's comprendre. teach? will have to look this one up*), to keep him, to familiarize herself with the cataclysm, to press herself to arrive at the terminal with him. She got out, the method opened itself, dictated.

·

van set, van wheat, van new, try to, try to aeon, try to do,
try to raw, try to cadre, try to sank, try to cease . . .

Homophonic translation can get me into meaning, away from the dangers of literal translation and into the space where language could play, could be nonsense, could be anything.

Mr. Dryden, I do not want to be, as a translator, a "Verbal Copyer." I agree, doing so "Tis much like dancing on Ropes with fetter'd Leggs."[6]

·

To extinguish (*atteindre could mean anything*) first off la guérite of the woman selling lottery tickets, flairer in an entaille the relentlessness of her bad luck, stationed on the side of the newspaper vendor's grotto, to present herself at the staircase of the Jaures metro after having traversed at three o'clock in the afternoon the cloistered passage of Villette Boulevard. (*or, Boulevard Villette. sounds better, sounds like Leduc's name*)

·

Not at my edge, but in anticipation.

·

Violette Leduc was an Aries, too. She wanted to throw a brick at every mirror she passed. In France, there are women who are belle, jolie, and laide. Leduc considered herself laide.

---

6. John Dryden, "From the Preface to Ovid's Epistles," in *The Translation Studies Reader*, 3rd Edition, ed. Lawrence Venuti (New York: Routledge, 2012), 39.

In Normandy during World War II, she was in love with the author Maurice Sachs. This love was one-sided, though Sachs probably appreciated the black-market food Violette gave him.

He yelled at her once, not in English, but translated as, "Your unhappy childhood is driving me to distraction. This afternoon you will take your basket, a pen and an exercise book ... [and] write down all the things you tell me."[7]

•

After reading Spivak, not one of my classmates felt up to the challenge of translation. It was easy to say, "We don't know enough," but how else were we to access the "seductions of translating," or the "responsibility to the trace of the other in the self?"[8]

I moved along, through the politics of translating European writers, women who fought in the French Resistance. Translation became a way to be close, to enter another time, to exist in a space of humility and discomfort.

"The task of the translator is to facilitate this love between the original and its shadow, a love that permits fraying, holds the agency of the translator and the demands of her imagined or actual audience at bay."[9]

•

The soil beneath my feet was packed down, hard as the sidewalk when I crossed it. Late August, but I remember being cold. Perhaps a shadow, the sun not high yet.

The register in the patisserie stood near the door. "Est-ce que je peux vous aider?" The woman seemed to be singing, but her mouth barely opened. She wore a striped sailor shirt and was smaller than I, fine boned, with closely cropped chestnut hair. Belle or jolie. Ironically, it felt as though she took up the whole room, as though she had arms long enough to grab anything she wanted without moving the rest of her body.

I said, "Un moment," without singing. *Je voudrais un . . .*

---

7. "Leduc, Violette," *Biography Reference Bank*, World Authors, 1950-70, Web, 9 Dec 2014.
8. Gayatri Chakravorty Spivak, "The Politics of Translation," in Venuti, 312.
9. Ibid., 313.

"Prenez votre temps."

•

Once I dreamed I was an old woman sitting on a plain dining room chair in a bare white room with windows on all sides. Sunlight gushed into the room and made it difficult, painful even, to open my eyes. This is like something. This image. Like something when I translate.

Beautiful and terrifying as the light changes.

•

This love between the original and its shadow could be the love of a parent for a child, for a lover, for an idea. Translation helps love become more real and less literal.

•

The Trot

FRENCH[10]	ENGLISH
Le fracas	To crash, to fall with; din; roar
Remua (v. remuer)	To move; to twitch
Les graines (n.)	Grains; specks (as in dust)
Tombèrent (v. tomber)	To fall (over or down)
S'habituait (trans. v. se habituer)	To accustom; get used to
L'envahiseur (n.)	Invader (n.); invading (adj.)
Secouait (v. secouer)	To shake; to shake off (oppression)
Heures creuses (n. + adj.)	Off-peak hours; slack; low season
Heures de pointe (n. + adj.)	Peak period; rush hour
Revoir (v.)	To see again; to meet again
Attendre (v.)	To wait; to wait for

---

10. Marianne Durand et al., *Collins Robert French Unabridged Dictionary*, 9th ed. (New York: Harper Collins, 2010.)

Suivre (v.)	To follow
Apprendre (v.)	To learn (how to do something)
Retenir (v.)	To hold back; to keep (garder)
Se familiariser (trans. v.)	To familiarize; get acquainted; to get to know
Cateclysme (n.)	Cataclysm
Se presser (trans. v.), or . . .	To press; to squeeze; to hurry
Terminus (n.)	Terminus; last stop
La méthode (n.)	Method
Dictait (v. dicter)	Dictate; lay down (as in steps)
Atteindre (v.)	To reach; to get at; to arrive
D'abord (n., adv.?)	Aboard
La guérite (n.)	Workman's hut; site office; sentry box
La vendeuse (n.)	Salesclerk; seller; vendor
Billets de loterie (n.)	Lottery tickets; raffle tickets
Flairer (v.)	To smell; to sniff, to sense
Entaille (n.)	Cut (gash or nick); notch, groove
Le relent (n.)	Foul smell; stench
La malchance (n.)	Bad luck; misfortune
Stationer (n.)	To be parked; to stay/remain (person)
La grotte (n.)	Cave; grotto
Le marchand de journaux (n.)	Newsdealer; newspaper seller/agent
Se presenter à (trans. v.)	To go in for; to sit (exam); to enter
L'escalier (n.)	Stairs; steps; stairway
Traversé (v. traverser)	To cross; to go through (port/tunnel)
Le passage (n.)	Passage; arcade; way; alleyway
Clouté (adj.)	Studded; hobnailed

•

Trot:

"A gait of a quadruped, originally of a horse, between walking and running, in which the legs move in diagonal pairs almost together, so that in a slow trot there is always one foot at least on the ground, but in a fast trot one pair leaves the ground before the other reaches it, all four feet being thus momentarily off the ground at once; hence applied to a similar gait of a man (or other biped), between a walk and a run . . ."[11]

11. "trot, no. 1." *OED Online*. Oxford University Press, December 2014. Web. 11 Dec 2014.

•

The dictionary steadies and unsteadies me. My body turns to the right and left, coiling and uncoiling as I look for words, find them, turn and write them down. The very touch of my shirt irritates me. It is always like this, the disappointment of not knowing, of having overreached my own grasp of French.

The dictionary's pages are thin, the words organized in various shades of gray, black, and blue. The sound of the pages flipping and flopping, like a pigeon puffing up and out its wings, provides pleasure. Pleasure in the feel of paper and the sound it makes in a search, this afternoon, for words.

•

"Je voudrais un sandwich, s'il vous plait." Robotic speech.
"Très bien. Lequel?"
I pointed.
"Celui la?" she asked.
"Oui."

I walked out of the patisserie quickly, smiling. The bench was still free. I sat down and peeled the plastic wrap off the sandwich. Sweet brown bread full of mayonnaisey, shredded carrots.

•

French/English/English/French. Moving between languages, a new picture of Leduc's text moves in, replacing details of what I'd imagined the words and sentences to mean. The table is no longer overthrown. A grain is a grain or a speck. Not a seed. That has been confirmed, as barley and wheat are off the table. Pun intended. Trains, timetables, rush hour, a city with newspaper sellers and lottery tickets. Metro stop and a street I came to know as an au pair in Paris.

How does delight replace my frustration so quickly? Why does the frustration return just as fast? Up and down. Up and down. The pleasure when I see possibility. The puckered mouth when I think, "How could you forget the word for stench?"

As important: Does the woman wait for a man, a boy, a father? Does she await a masculine noun?

•

Twenty-four, twenty-five, twenty-six, twenty-seven, twenty-eight, twenty-nine, thirty, thirty-one, thirty-two, thirty-three, thirty-four, thirty-five, thirty-six . . . the crash. The table moved, grains/crumbs fell into her skirt.

She was not accustomed to the invader/invading. It shook her every five minutes during off-peak hours, every two minutes during peak times. To meet again, to wait, to follow, to learn, to hold back, to familiarize herself with the cataclysm, to make herself arrive at the last stop with it. She left, the method opened itself, dictated. To arrive (*word choice*) aboard (*look this up; it sounds weird, but don't try to domesticate it*) the lottery ticket seller's kiosk, to smell in the notch/groove the stench of bad luck, to park herself beside the newsdealer's grotto (*can't mean grotto; has to be something else*) hole, to enter the stairway of the Jaurès Metro after having gone through, at three in the afternoon, the studded passage of Boulevard Villette.

•

Violette, are we close? I feel close. You died six years before I was born. You wrote novels, tracked, devotedly Simone de Beauvoir, sold black-market goods in a country I would travel to twenty-four years after your death. See—vingt-quatre, twenty-four—it's a sign.

The numbers run up and up. The paranoid counting. Why is the woman counting? Who is the woman who is counting? She waits and the seconds between the crashes, the minutes when shaken, divide the time. Heartbeats. Tapping feet. The line of infinitive verbs paired with masculine direct objects, the "re" at the end of these verbs digs in. Not a knife, but perhaps a cigarette being snuffed out beneath the sole of someone's shoe.

Are they bombs? What moved the table, and also what kind of skirt?

I am going to leave out some definite articles. I am going to change things. The scurrying tone, the counting and panic need some help. Crumbs underscore poverty. Should the invader become "him" or "it"?

A journey to hide from the invader, but a journey down into the metro. Bomb shelter?

But sound nice. Have poetry,
or sing.

•

The sandwich made me sad. It didn't look any good. Not like what I'd seen everyone else leaving with. Those customers had words to ask for things I might actually want to eat.

•

renard: (n.m.) fox, fox fur
Is she a woman wearing a fox fur?
I don't want Google to tell me,
but it might be so.

•

Twenty-four, twenty-five, twenty-six, twenty-seven, twenty-eight, twenty-nine, thirty, thirty-one, thirty-two, thirty-three, thirty-four, thirty-five, thirty-six . . . the crash. The table moved, crumbs fell into her skirt.

She was not accustomed to the invading. It shook her every five minutes during off-peak hours, every two minutes during peak times. To meet it again, to wait, to follow, to learn, to hold it back, to familiarize herself with the cataclysm, to force herself to arrive at the last stop in time. She left, the method opened itself to her, dictated. To reach first the lottery ticket seller's kiosk, to smell the stench of bad luck in the groove, to park herself beside the newsdealer's hole, to enter the stairway of the Jaurès Metro after having gone through, at three in the afternoon, the rough passage of Boulevard de la Villette.

•

The sandwich wasn't delicious, but it was very—

Google tells me "passage clouté" means crosswalk, so I will make it, "after having gone through, at three in the afternoon, the Boulevard de la Villette crosswalk."

If I say crossed the crosswalk, so many crosses make too much—

•

She was not accustomed to the invading. It shook her every five minutes during off-peak hours, every two minutes during peak times. To meet again, to wait, to follow, to learn, to hold back, to familiarize herself with the cataclysm, to force herself to arrive at the last stop with him. She left, the method opened itself to her, dictated. To reach first the lottery ticket seller's kiosk, to smell the stench of bad luck in the groove, to park herself beside the newsdealer's hole, to enter the stairway of metro Jaurès after having traversed, at three in the afternoon, the crosswalk at Boulevard de la Villette.

•

avec lui—I recognized the potential for an object of desire—*with him*

Translation Folio

KARL KROLOW

Translator's Introduction

Stuart Friebert

I MET KARL KROLOW IN the early 60s, when he read for a group of Oberlin students of German I was accompanying on the way to a summer session in Vienna. Not a day has gone by since without my reading around in his magisterial oeuvre—poems, prose, translations, criticism, memoir—the dimensions and depths of which few writers have equaled, and translating yet another of his more than three thousand poems, many under his direct supervision. One of my most cherished possessions is his note saying "you have my permission to translate anything you are drawn to." "Drawn" indeed, the key to opening the first door in his many-roomed mansion.

Full disclosure: that he should have done so, as well as written the afterword to my first German book of poems, not to mention inspired three others, is quintessential Krolow, who more than any other writer I know went WAY out of his way to lend a hand to anyone seeking his counsel and support—especially younger writers who were nowhere near being taken seriously and might well never have been. As a critic, a reader, a judge of literary competitions, and especially as president of The German Academy of Language and Literature (1972-75), Krolow did more than any other writer of his generation to shape and nurture the talents of others.

As one who was beginning to be taken seriously in some quarters, however, but who was also on the verge of being cast out of the "den" altogether by some shameless critics and mendacious writers, Paul Celan would likely never have attained the stature and regard we pay him now without Krolow's intercession at a critical juncture in Germany's post-WWII history. Some argue that Krolow was "merely" trying to atone for his having remained in Germany during the Nazi years, and not having risked speaking out against atrocities many surely sensed if not knew were being committed. That is not a stone to cast, many of us believe, who read "the record" differently.

In all the work, what impresses most, perhaps, (as I've written elsewhere) is Krolow's range across many subjects and themes, even as he absorbs and articulates them by means of lyric voices that are at once abstract and detached, but so concentrated and focused that what is observed becomes sometimes unbearably voyeuristic. As he explores the sum and substance of our private and public lives, Krolow's signature paradox is that the more detached the texts seem, the more intimately the reader is affected. Krolow put it this way: "Poems are for those waiting for lightning."

KARL KROLOW : Four Poems

Earlier

There were just fingers,
which caught spiders' legs,
earlier, earlier, when nails
were still not cracked,
and I imitated the bird,
which no one called by name.
Stand still a moment!
You wore a very particular dress,
a beckoning carnation
between your lips,
earlier, when they said "Love Love."
You cast no shadow any longer,
when you became unfaithful
and the old time suddenly
ticked differently.
Other pulses.
It ran down without shadows.
We were lucky
that nothing happened,
when we waited for
the lightning to tear us apart.

What Else Do You Want

What else do you want?
You've come along another day
and live:
as if this life
were nothing special,
light behind your eyes and in your head,
which you don't understand as it is:
an eternal film with you
and others: words, magic,
most of all astonishment.
There's you different each time and that's how
you were exactly, did some things as if just for fun:
another day, an index in any case
for existence. Yet you know:
Death never asks: may I go then?
He remains unquestionably. You'd
wanted nothing from him.
Which told him to remain.
You can't do anything
but live on with his feints,
spared, with good behavior
and quiet from day to day
his question in your ear,
one never asked,
as long as you live.

I've Had Enough

I've had
enough of the succession of things.
Contemporaneity
perplexes me
like natural good luck
or sitting at a
long table without end,
which loses itself in the landscape,
there where illusion begins.
I've had enough
of being stood around by life.
It gapes.
It tears the clothes off my body.
I've had enough
of being naked that way,
with assiduity and bodily imperfections,
with decay, the smell
of rotting gall-nuts.
I want to be alone
with the cut in my vein.
I've had enough
of feeling the ripple
of my soul in my back
and being asked
about its origin.
Muzzle me
before I say a word.

Good Night

This definitive spring, nights.
Only white teeth shine.
That can't be said in any
language. The logic of bodies
is stronger: a music in every
moment, like a hand,
which grips beneath a shoulder,
another life in any case.
perhaps a necessary
preparation for death,
all that without fear, a garland,
because it's May and everywhere
there's crackling, for happiness.
What is love?
La douce pensee.
Werther is far off. How much sleeplessness!
The Osram lamps glow
for Phaedra. Good night, good night.

Translated from the German by Stuart Friebert

GERRI BRIGHTWELL

The Joke

As soon as he learned that Kaufman was dead Christophe hurried to the bus station. During the hours it took to reach his home town he ate his way through a packet of biscuits that left crumbs on his coat and inside his undershirt so that, when finally he undressed that night, he found them caught in his chest hair, in his navel, in the dark hair of his crotch like a pale infestation.

The bus was old. When it rained, water leaked in from the ventilation hatches and dripped on an old woman across the aisle. She tied a scarf over her head and when she saw Christophe watching she gave him a sad smile. He looked away to the window where condensation had fogged the glass and rubbed a hole with his fingertip. He bent his eye towards it but now that they'd left the city the view was always the same: green hills, dingy houses like old teeth, fields where cattle stood sullen in the rain, and everywhere mud that darkened fields and paths or even the occasional fresh grave in a churchyard. The sight of those graves sent a thrill through Christophe's gut. Kaufman—buried now, and serve him right.

Christophe was a clerk in a government office. His supervisor had been off for nearly a week with the flu and when Christophe had called in that morning, his voice purposefully weak and punctuated by coughs, the secretary had interrupted to tell him he should do everyone a favor and stay home. Scarcely able to believe his luck, Christophe grabbed his coat and umbrella and raced down to the foyer where he stood buttoning his coat. Just beyond the glass, rain was slanting across the street. When he stepped outside the wind pushed his umbrella inside out and the rain lashed at him as he struggled to right it. Twice that happened so at the corner he dumped the umbrella in a dustbin and strode on with his head bowed against the downpour, all the way to the huge old edifice that housed the bus station. What a day for a journey as though, even dead and buried, Kaufman was determined to plague him.

An early November morning but the bus station was far from empty. The wind gusted through an open archway and slapped rain onto the ground with a heartlessness that made Christophe shiver. He joined a queue to buy a ticket at a small barred window then sat on a bench, the ticket already turning soft with damp between his fingers and his fingers restless, turning it over and over. His coat gave off a wet wool smell that mixed sickeningly with the stink of piss and diesel rising off the concrete. He lit a cigarette and breathed in its smoke, closing his eyes and letting it drift from his nose, and it warmed him a little, or he thought it did.

When at last the cigarette had burnt down to its filter he crushed it beneath his shoe and glanced at the clock above the ticket office. Nearly half an hour until the bus was due to leave. It had pulled in already, one of several dirty green buses lined up along the bay, number 51 showing through its windscreen. A few people gathered around as if the driver might let them on early, though of course he didn't, shutting the doors behind him with a hiss then striding away towards the staffroom. Once there had been a waiting room for passengers but the window had been painted over years ago and now a sign on the door said NO ADMITTANCE.

Christophe lit another cigarette and smoked it quickly then dug in his pocket for change. At a kiosk he bought a paper cup of tea, a meat pie, a packet of dry biscuits, a bottle of mineral water. He'd left his flat in such a hurry he hadn't eaten breakfast—a cup for tea ready on the kitchen table, the remains of a loaf set out beside a pot of jam, everything as it had been when he'd turned to the obituaries: a small indistinct photograph of a mild-looking man in his fifties, but it was Kaufman alright. Long-time schoolteacher in Christophe's home town, son of a renowned physicist—Christophe hadn't known that, but he didn't read on. Already his head was hissing, his mouth dry, and he dropped the paper onto the table and hurried away for his coat.

He didn't buy another newspaper in the bus station. In fact he hurried past the kiosk selling papers and magazines and cheap novels and waited impatiently by the bus, eating his pie, sipping his tea, shifting from foot to foot in the cold until the driver returned and took everyone's tickets. Usually for bus journeys he equipped himself with something to read but this time he lit a cigarette and settled into his seat with the bottle of water cradled against his soft belly, watching the city streets sweep past, then the factories by the river, then the relentless countryside, and even when he opened the biscuits and slowly ate his way through them (despite them being as dry as old dirt) he didn't open the water because he'd long ago made up his mind what his revenge would be.

After the first few hours sitting felt like hard work. His knees had gone stiff, his buttocks were sore, and the air smelled of wet clothes, and unwashed bodies, and the sulfurous hard-boiled eggs that the old lady across the aisle ate one after the other, pulling them from her basket and making them vanish whole into her mouth like a magician. At last Christophe closed his eyes as though he might sleep.

•

THE WINTER CHRISTOPHE HAD TURNED fifteen a terrible cold had fallen over the eastern part of the country. It had weighed down everything—the ducks struggling flat-footed over frozen ponds, the tails of smoke lingering above chimneys, the ragged breath of sheep and cows huddled in the snow. Frost furred power lines and telephone lines and washing lines; it gathered along doors and windows where moisture was wrung from warm air. Stepping outside was like being catapulted into a future in which this planet would be nothing but a rock hurtling around a dying sun.

Christophe would rather have stayed inside with his mother and sisters but being a boy he was obliged to help his father. The two of them chopped up a spruce that had come down in a windstorm and stacked the firewood by the backdoor, and when his father—a doctor—drove out to see his patients, Christophe went with him to sit in the driver's seat while his father went inside, touching his foot to the accelerator whenever the engine stuttered. How miserable it was waiting there with the cold pressing in through the glass and only the radio for company. Even with the heater set to high and his pajamas bulky beneath his clothes, he shivered right down to his bones. As for the radio, the frigid air meant that most stations warped and wobbled or hissed with static, and he was left listening to government broadcasts of classical music. How surprised he was, though, at the way an opera singer's voice could swell against the inside of the car. He'd bend his whole self towards the radio as though the voice might warm him and hummed along, his breath hanging in the air like ghosts. The whole time he watched the door through which his father had vanished, hoping that the fever had come down, or the laceration be a shallow one, or the dying man die quickly.

The intense cold lasted eight days. On the ninth Christophe woke in the darkness to the phone ringing and his father's hushed voice. He was about to swing his legs out of bed when he noticed a soft clatter on the roof just above him: rain. With relief he huddled back under the covers. A few minutes later his father shook him. A patient on the far side of town. Christophe was all outrage—Why did he need him when it was raining? Besides, the girls got to stay home, and two of them were older than him, and the holidays were nearly over—but his father tore the blankets from his bed and told him to hurry.

In the darkness everything glinted wetly: the road, the smooth tops of cars, the spiked railings around houses. His father drove barely faster than walking pace and hunched close to the wheel, his breath whistling through his teeth when the car slid, as it did at even the gentlest touch of the brakes. The windscreen wipers squawked and left smears of ice that blurred the streetlights. On the main square they passed a car that had slid sideways into a lamppost, and a few minutes later a van that had missed the narrow bridge over the river and now sat nose down on the bank as though about to plunge through the ice.

Christophe and his father might have made it to whoever had called on that godforsaken night if it hadn't been for a dog running into the road. Instinctively his father's foot pressed the brake pedal and the car slewed around, dragged by its own weight, the headlights catching a confusion of hedges and gates and houses. A lurch, a roar of the engine, and Christophe was thrown so hard his breath jerked out of him in a grunt. He registered the sickening sound of living bone hitting something unyielding, then all was still.

He waited for the shock of pain. He couldn't move, couldn't do more than listen to the thud of blood through his ears and raindrops crackling against the roof. Through the windscreen there was nothing except the blue darkness of snow pushed up against the glass. His chest hurt and his breathing was coming roughly—but that was only his seatbelt pulled tight across his chest and holding him up against the tilt of the car. With his teeth he yanked off his gloves then fumbled for the release. He didn't think to brace himself and fell against the dashboard.

Only now did he glance at his father. He was slumped over the steering wheel, his hat missing, the hairless skin of his crown pale in the darkness. Christophe touched his arm and it swung loose like a dead man's. A fizz of shock rushed through him though he knew his father wasn't dead, or most likely wasn't at least.

He tried the door but the snow held it shut. Instead he wound down his window and heaved himself out into the snowbank where he floundered, sinking, snow in his clothes and cold everywhere, until at last he managed to crawl to the roadside and stood there huffing onto his bare hands. Across the road stood a row of old houses with walled gardens and tall metal gates. From the closest a rind of light showed around the shutters and smoke hung in the dark sky above its chimney. Christophe started towards it but the moment he stepped onto the road the world toppled over. A pop somewhere inside in his shoulder, a sudden uprush of pain. He lay still while rain dripped onto his face, his ear, through his hair, and the pain pulsed and pulsed then sank away. When he got back onto his feet he clutched his shoulder though he knew it was only bruised and shuffled towards the gate in tiny steps.

The metal bars were icy against his bare hands but at least the gate swung open. He was near enough now to catch the busy mumble of an orchestra and a baritone voice lifting above it, surging and distant and quite unearthly at this time of night. He climbed the front steps and heard another sound, strange raw gasps from much closer. He stood with his hand raised and listened: Was it a woman crying? Was it laughter? It so unnerved him that he knocked and it stopped instantly. He knocked again, he even pushed his face up to the wood and shouted, "Please help—my father's hurt. He's the doctor." The house stood silent. Rain chattered onto the gravel and the wind shushed it, and when he stepped back and tilted his head he heard the singing again caught up in the wind, the melody so close to familiar that he took a breath to hum a little then stopped himself: his father was lying injured and unattended in the car. Christophe knew about head injuries, he knew about hypothermia—with a doctor for a father, how could he not?

The rain was coming down harder now. He took the path around the house meaning to rap on the shutters except here the music was more distinct and he followed it on into the shadows calling, "Hello? Hello?" Across a small courtyard stood the low shape of what must once have been a stable. A fan of light lit the wet gravel where someone had left the door ajar and from it surged the hectic rush of the orchestra and that soaring baritone. The door was so close he reached it in a few steps and knocked. He called out too, for all the good it would do, then heaved the door open.

In the rush and roar of the music Christophe couldn't make sense of what he was looking at: under the shabby light of a single bulb a man in short-sleeves was standing on a crate, his back to the door, the loose loops of his braces hanging down by his thighs as though he'd started undressing and changed his mind. Christophe came closer and shouted and only now did the man turn, his face twisted in surprise. A thin face, the eyes deepset, the brown hair cut so short the bones of his head showed through. Christophe recognized him: Mr. Kaufman, the school chemistry teacher. He'd moved to town only the year before, a humorless stick of a man who went about his teaching mechanically and seemed barely to occupy his own person. There'd been talk of bad luck—a baby born sick and soon dying, his wife being shut away for months in a sanatorium—and even if it wasn't true, certainly an air of misery clung to him. At the school it didn't make him an object of sympathy or pity but rather a man to be avoided, as though in his pain he could lash out at any moment and the boys be made to suffer.

Now Kaufman's shirt was unbuttoned at the neck and in his bony hands he held a length of rope, poised to throw it up to the rafters. Seeing Christophe his mouth shut fast, then he tossed the rope away across the floor and lowered himself to sit on the crate. He hid his face in his hands. When Christophe bellowed above the music, "Sir? It's my father—the car went off the road," Kaufman didn't look up. Christophe added, "He's hurt. He needs help. Please, sir."

When at last Kaufman raised his head, how tired he looked—the skin around his eyes puckered, his eyes watery, his mouth a crooked line. He pushed himself off the crate like an old man and walked heavy-footed to a table where a large radio sat. The hugeness of the music vanished and in the silence his shoes scraped back across the floor. A few feet from Christophe he ran a hand down his face. "My boy—" he said. His voice sounded half-drowned, dragged from somewhere deep inside. "My boy," and he shook his head sadly, then heaved in a breath. "Yes, I'll come . . . But please . . . allow me . . . " He stood with one hand on his cheek, the other against his chest, looking around him as though he'd been startled awake. Then he fetched his jacket from a sawhorse and pulled it on awkwardly, like a man helping another man into his clothes, and shooed Christophe to the doorway. There he stopped the boy with the weight of his hand on his shoulder. When Christophe looked up Kaufman's mouth made a wet clacking as he tried to say something, his tongue loose, feeling its way around his mouth before he managed, "Boy—you're not one to talk, are you?"

"No," Christophe said quickly, though it wasn't until that moment that he let himself quite understand: the crate, the rope, Kaufman alone with the opera raging around him, and now his fingers clenching the bruised flesh of Christophe's shoulder. He wouldn't let himself pull away. He wouldn't even let himself turn his head because that "No," wasn't enough, it had already been swallowed by the air between them and still Kaufman held him, his eyes even in the near-dark soft and terrible and Christophe, who wanted nothing more than to free himself and run to where his father lay injured, blurted, "You can trust me absolutely sir, really you can, I won't tell a soul, I promise."

In the following weeks he'd wonder if he'd said it so quickly, so earnestly, that he'd stirred Kaufman's distrust, though as soon as the words left his mouth he realized he meant them. Held there in Kaufman's grip he was more than a mere schoolboy: the two of them were fellow souls in a cruel world, they understood each other in a way they might never again. The very idea of it rushed hot and clean through his chest.

At last Kaufman had let his hand drop and Christophe had said, "My father, sir," and hurried away down the driveway with Kaufman behind him. At the gate the two of them had pulled off their shoes to cross the slick road in their socks, and they'd found Christophe's father struggling to haul himself clear of the snow beside the tipped-up car. Together they'd helped him into the house where he was laid on a sofa and blankets brought, and brandy, Mrs. Kaufman watching from the doorway in her dressing gown, her face gaunt, her eyes raw and surprised as though she'd just been slapped, not uttering a word while Kaufman was all gentle solicitude.

The cold settled in again for the last few days of the holidays, not as severely as before but grim nonetheless. Christophe and his sisters crept about like burglars with no friends over to play, no radio to cheer the house because upstairs their father was lying in bed with the curtains drawn until his bruised brain healed. It was up to Christophe to chop firewood and bring it inside but once that was done his mother didn't complain if he folded himself into an armchair by the fire. He'd lay a book on his knees and have every intention of reading, yet within minutes his attention would slip away. He'd see Kaufman on that crate about to fling the rope above his head and horror would strike him once more that a man should feel such pain, that a man could suffer so—losing his child, being bound to a wife who'd lost herself in grief—and he'd turn on the radio very low and search the stations for the wild flinging of the soul onto the air that he'd heard that night in Kaufman's outbuilding, and when he did find an opera he'd crouch with his ear up against the speaker and let a quivering warmth bloom inside him, a feeling of tenderness for that man he'd never much liked but who was a human being like himself suffering unbearable pain, and whom he'd saved—yes, saved—though quite by accident.

Such a feeling was hard to hold on to. He'd hear his mother or sisters coming up the corridor and snap off the radio, and when he hurried back to his armchair and stared down at his book the sympathy he'd conjured up would vanish beneath what else he remembered of that night: Kaufman's hand gripping his sore shoulder, the awful undertone of pleading when he said, "Boy—you're not one to talk, are you?" Soon he'd be imagining what he'd have found if he'd walked into that outbuilding a few minutes later: the violence of the music, the rope creaking from the slight motion of the body, the air reeking of emptied bowels, and Kaufman not a man any more but a monstrous thing hanging there.

He spent so much time thinking about what Kaufman had nearly done that the idea of seeing him again made him nervous. Luckily on the first morning of the new term there were so many boys crowding through the doors that Christophe's unease fell away and, seeing Kaufman standing in his usual place on the main stairs, he lifted his head and gave him a small smile. When Kaufman stared back blankly—maybe he hadn't noticed Christophe in the crowd—he hurried off and only looked back when he was nearly through the cloakroom doorway. There was Kaufman, head awkwardly turned to keep Christophe in sight, his shoulders high and his thin face hard with fury. Christophe's throat tightened: all those times he'd crouched by the radio searching for that surge of joy at how he'd saved a man; all those times he'd disgusted himself picturing Kaufman's body dangling above the crate—all of it felt laid bare now. He ducked away and clumsily pushed through a knot of boys into the cloakroom.

That lunchtime he squeezed in with some friends at one of the long dining tables, and naturally their talk turned to the chaos caused by the freezing rain. One boy described his dog skittering over the road, another how his grandfather had stepped onto their doorstep in his dressing gown and fallen with such force his legs were thrown into the air and revealed that underneath he was utterly naked. Not only that but the poor man had hurt his back and couldn't get up, so he had to lie there exposed until the boy's mother heard his cries for help. Christophe made himself laugh though all he could think about was his father's head thudding against the steering wheel, and how he'd gone for help only to find Kaufman preparing to hang himself. Soon the story was over but Christophe was laughing so hard his eyes were watering and his face was red, and he bawled, "Christ, having to save a man like that. Oh my God, that's so awful." The boy beside him elbowed him and Christophe shoved him back, and it wasn't until the boy hissed, "Shhh," that he looked up and he saw why the others had fallen silent: Kaufman. His head was tilted at an odd angle and his face had turned the white of a boiled potato.

He knew immediately how Kaufman could have misunderstood his words and a nauseating cold sank through his belly. In a panic he started to get up then sat down again with his head hung low. "What in God's name is this all about?" Kaufman barked, and Christophe bit his lip. One of the other boys spoke up: "The icestorm, sir. We were just having a laugh, sir, that's all." Kaufman spat, "At whose expense? With you lot, it's always at someone's expense." None of the boys said a word. The boy whose grandfather had fallen scratched at something on the tabletop—how could he repeat that story to a teacher when his grandfather was on the town council?

Cottony spit had gathered at the corners of Kaufman's mouth. He snapped, "Stand against the wall, the lot of you, and not another word or you'll all get detention." None of them moved: the dining hall was loud with voices and laughter, it always was, then Kaufman seized Christophe by his jacket and hauled him off the bench, and in an instant the other boys had lined up facing the wall, hands behind their backs like prisoners about to be shot, and there they stood for the half hour until the bell rang and when it did they skulked off without a word.

Christophe didn't have chemistry until the end of the next afternoon. He took a seat in the back by the window but Kaufman pointed at the workbench in front of him: "You—here where I can keep an eye on you." He had to sit next to a thuggish boy who broke pipettes and scorched his wooden test-tube holders and spilled acid in a soapy patch on the floor. To Christophe's surprise, although he'd have sworn Kaufman had seen who'd upset the acid, he was made to mop it up. At the end of class when a knot of boys gathered at the sink and a retort was smashed against the tap, Kaufman didn't bother to come over to investigate but blamed Christophe, as though he simply needed a culprit. As punishment Christophe was ordered to stay behind to scrub glassware. Thankfully Kaufman shut himself in his study and only occasionally glanced at him through the small window into the laboratory until, well after six o'clock, he came out and jerked his thumb towards the door. When Christophe got home his parents were beside themselves. His mother snatched him to her chest and breathed hard into his hair and his father, an uncommonly decent man, listened to his explanation of being unfairly blamed and kept saying, "Mr. Kaufman? Are you sure? He seems such an innocuous fellow."

From then on Christophe was blamed for outbreaks of laughter during assembly, a washbasin tap broken off in the junior toilets and the floor being flooded, the scrawling of obscenities on the library wall. It wasn't just Kaufman who picked on Christophe but the other teachers too, as if Kaufman had revealed another side to him that somehow they'd overlooked, and while it wasn't uncommon for teachers to single out one pupil as a troublemaker and to punish him out of all proportion—it was even accepted as a way to discourage others from misbehaving—usually such scapegraces were boys already trailing a reputation for waywardness.

Of course it was unfair and Christophe's father, for all that he'd protested that there must have been some misunderstanding, that Mr. Kaufman was surely a gentle soul, eventually went to talk to the principal. The principal assured him that since his teachers wouldn't punish a boy without good reason Christophe must be guilty, and wouldn't he prefer that his son's misbehavior be stamped out now before it grew more serious?

Kaufman haunted Christophe's dreams: a stumbling creature pursuing him through the school corridors, or lying in wait in the darkness behind an abandoned house. He'd wake with his pajamas sticking to his chest and his heart frantic. He'd snap on the light and try to turn his mind to more pleasant things, but he couldn't prize his thoughts away from Kaufman: how he'd get his revenge on him one day, and how Kaufman would be revealed for the weak-willed and spiteful man he was. He'd piece together how it would play out: Kaufman blaming him for an offense so absurd that even the principal protested, and this time he would look into the matter and discover that it was another boy entirely—or perhaps even Kaufman himself!—who'd smashed the laboratory equipment, or carved smutty images onto the main doors of the school; or maybe Christophe would catch Kaufman in some wrongdoing, nude photographs of women hidden in his office, maybe, and Kaufman's career would end in disgrace. Christophe could picture it: the principal bellowing at Kaufman and Kaufman's face a ghastly white, how he'd hurry out the gates for the last time to the jeering of the boys. What was less clear was how Christophe would convince anyone to believe him.

Late one afternoon when Christophe was sitting in the eerie quiet of the laboratory writing his laboratory report for the third time—Kaufman had thrown it in his face, and it was true that it was a mess of inaccuracies and unfinished thoughts—the secretary hurried in and summoned Kaufman away. During all of the detentions Christophe had served, Kaufman had watched him through the small window from his study. How odd it was to sit shivering (the heating had been turned down for the night) under the gaze of nothing worse than an empty square of light. He scratched his nose with the end of his pen and stared at what he'd written, all of those dead sentences laid out across the page. He couldn't think what one might conclude from the presence of this particular metal during this particular reaction. He slouched and propped his head on his hand. He yawned and let himself fart; he even got up and walked about to relieve the stiffness in his back from sitting so long on a stool, and still Kaufman didn't return. Fifteen minutes passed. Christophe strolled about with his fingers trailing the smooth tops of the workbenches then, as though he'd simply been waiting for the right moment, he let himself into Kaufman's study.

In there it was warmer and the light had a gentle butteriness to it. Christophe touched Kaufman's office chair, a leather thing that spun easily, then he sat in it and swung himself around, legs hooked beneath the seat so as not to knock anything over. The office whirled around him: the small window, the filing cabinet, the shelves with their bottles and jars and piles of papers, the doorway, the small window again. Through the glass the laboratory looked bleak and far away.

Afterwards he could not have said what made him open the desk drawers—a sense, perhaps, that spinning in the chair was the behavior of a child when he was fifteen and nearly a man, that he was throwing away his one chance to act. Even months later when he was living in the city with his grandparents he'd remember the angry excitement in his chest as his hands rooted through the drawers with their papers and pens, their rubber bands and paperclips, how he'd pushed his fingers to their gritty far corners; he'd remember the moment his fingertips touched the crisp corner of an envelope and how his breathing had quickened as he pulled it out: a letter, and what a secret it turned out to hold—enough, in the months that followed, to make him wish himself back to that chilly laboratory, to wish that he'd stayed at his workbench finishing his report; enough to make Kaufman, unable to reveal the theft without explaining what was missing, to vandalize his own office and blame Christophe, and for Christophe to be expelled for the broken window and bottles, and for the books with their pages torn out and covered with piss on the floor; it was enough, finally, for Christophe to be sent to the city to attend a rather inferior school that accepted troublesome boys, and for him to become a clerk in an unimportant government office when he'd always imagined he'd be so much more.

•

WHEN HE OPENED HIS EYES condensation had thickened on the bus window and he wiped at it with his knuckle. Rivulets of rain quivered over the glass like live things, jostled by the air as the bus rushed on towards the town. Except, Christophe realized, the bus had slowed, and when he leaned close to the glass he glimpsed a plain grey steeple high on the hillside, its shape as familiar as his own hand. He snatched up his bottle of water and twisted off the cap. The water was warm and tasted of plastic but he drank down half then took a breath and kept drinking, even when he noticed an uncomfortable pressure in his bladder. Funny, all of a sudden he felt grubby from the dampness, the dirty seat cushions, the rancid stink of tobacco and his own clothes that he'd sweated into and that, now that he looked down, were speckled with pale crumbs from the biscuits he'd eaten. He worked his tongue around his mouth: a pasty residue was caught between his teeth, gritty and slightly sweet.

The bus slowed for the narrow bridge over the river and edged along so close to the parapet that Christophe braced himself for the squeal of metal against stone. A glimpse of the river—grey and wrinkled from the rain—then they were pulling into the town square and nervousness gripped him. His hand went to his pocket for his cigarettes but it was empty. He needed to relieve himself but he couldn't, not yet, and instead he squeezed in the sides of the empty water bottle, the plastic crackling in his hands as the bus swung around the square then, with almost a flourish, swerved to a halt outside the town hall.

He grabbed his bag and stood, expecting a rush of people down the aisle, but the bus was almost empty. A couple of teenagers in denim jackets slouched on the back seat, an old man who'd fallen asleep sat tilted into the aisle. Only a young woman got to her feet, pulling at the hand of a toddler and cradling a large bag in her other arm. Even the old woman who'd been eating eggs had gone.

It wasn't yet evening but the sky was low and an insistent rain was falling. The moment he stepped down from the bus it dripped through his hair and down his face, and he wished he hadn't ditched his umbrella after all. He looked about, squinting slightly. The town hall much the same as ever with its flag hanging limp, but from where a bakery and a greengrocer's had once stood came the fluorescent glare of lights—a supermarket, right on the main square and just beyond, vivid against the gloom, the neon green cross of a pharmacy. A little farther away the café that had been there for decades, where old men spent their days playing backgammon, looked dingy and deserted, never mind that the lights were on. A few hunched men sat smoking at their tables. Different old men from his time, Christophe thought, though they looked indistinguishable in their brown jackets and dark hats. By the window a bored young man in an apron stood looking out, his fingers tugging his mustache, and Christophe raised his hand to shield his face, ridiculously, because as he walked past he realized: this young man could have no idea who he was, it had been twenty years since he'd left and besides—what could it possibly mean to him, a boy having been expelled and sent away all those years ago?

The fullness in his bladder irritated him, despite him having planned things this way: no getting off the bus to take a piss for the last couple of hours, the bottle of water to drink shortly before arriving, though in truth he hadn't needed it and maybe it had been too much because now his trousers were tight around his belly. A cigarette would have helped, it would have calmed him, but he couldn't bear the thought of going into the supermarket or the café to buy more and instead he hurried away from the square.

In the rain the pavement seemed to ooze beneath his feet, just as it had on those days he'd walked home from school wet through, his bag heavy, so much homework that he knew he wouldn't have time for anything else until he went to sleep. There was the school on his right and he stared through the railings. Pale light showed through the windows where boys must have been sitting over their mathematics and their history and, at the far end of the building, their chemistry experiments. Everything else was grey: the stone walls, the concrete yard, all of it just as he remembered, and it seemed impossible that he should be back here, as though he'd broken through to the past and everything could be put to rights. But of course it couldn't. Once he'd been sent to the city his parents and sisters became little more than acquaintances, people who'd occasionally visit and urge him to come home for the holidays, and he'd refuse as though he couldn't bear to leave his grandparents when the truth was that he couldn't stand the idea of getting to know them all again as this lesser boy who'd never amount to much.

After a few years his grandparents had died and he'd inherited their flat, then his parents had died and his sisters moved away, and somehow twenty years had passed. When he thought about Kaufman—and in the beginning he'd thought about him constantly—it was with the wretched hope that he would kill himself after all, and when he thought about the night he'd come upon Kaufman standing on the crate, he pictured himself taking his time getting out of the car, or looking around for lights in the other houses. Sometimes he imagined how things would have been if his father hadn't been called out, or the dog not run into the street, because then Kaufman would simply have hanged himself after all, causing a scandal but one soon forgotten, his position filled by a new chemistry teacher and Christophe excelling in his classes, and going on to university, and becoming a doctor like his father.

Up ahead an estate agent's office had replaced the cobbler's shop and there were new signs directing traffic into a one-way system. Not much change for twenty years, not really, and those changes gave the town a toyish look: the bright colors of lit-up signs, a tiny roundabout where two roads met, all of it shining in the rain.

He took the street leading up the hill to the older part of town. He'd walked this hill hundreds of times as a boy but now the strain of the incline dragged at him. His bladder weighed him down, his chest burned. Soon he stopped and rested a hand against a lamppost to catch his breath. He wasn't an old man, he was barely middle-aged, but his belly had long ago turned soft and his thighs thickened. He ate what he liked and how much he liked, and since he lived on his own, what did it matter?

From here he could see the church again, stark against the sky. Not a beautiful building and certainly not elegant, so sturdily built it looked as though it were sinking into the ground beneath the weight of its massive walls, its tiny windows an afterthought. As he came in through the gate a yellow banner strung up over the door caught his eye, a call to salvation, and he sucked at his cheeks in annoyance. He patted his pocket for cigarettes before remembering he hadn't bought more, and he looked away over the churchyard, peering about him and sweeping one hand over his hair. It was so wet it clung to his fingers and he shivered. His coat was soaked, the legs of his trousers too, and though he was here in the churchyard at last, he felt cold and weary.

It shouldn't, he thought, be difficult to find the grave. After all, the graveyard wasn't so big, and fresh graves—well, how many could there be in a small town like this? He followed the path beneath trees whose roots had pushed old gravestones askew, then around to the back of the church where the newer graves would be. By the fence a small backhoe was sitting with the tip of its muddy bucket touching the ground in benediction and against it a man was leaning, wiping mud off a spade with a rag. In the turf close by, crowded in against the fence, lay a long heap of dirt with garlands and bouquets slung over it, all sodden from the rain. Christophe stopped, about to turn back, to go into the church to wait, never mind that his bladder was piercingly full. The smell of wet earth was everywhere, a mineral smell with a tinge of rot. He'd expected something different: the grave covered with turf, a gravestone that his piss would splash against, the utter relief that would run through him.

The workman lifted his head. "Funeral's long over." His voice came out muffled, as though there were something wrong with his tongue.

"D'you know who's buried here?"

Bright beads of rain clung to the brim of the man's hardhat, and when he shrugged they fell away. "God knows," he said. "I just dig the hole then fill it in. Once you're dead you're dead. You want to pray for their souls, it doesn't matter which grave you're standing at."

"I'm looking for someone. Kaufman."

The man shrugged again. "Could be here. Could be the protestant place on the edge of town. Then again, there's people nowadays prefer cremation, or have relatives who want to save money and leave them in one of those highrise burial niches. That's not being buried, if you ask me, it's being shelved."

Christophe stepped closer. "Are there cards?"

"There's always cards. Go ahead and look if it means so much to you."

He turned away with his spade and rag, as if out of discretion, and Christophe stepped up to the freshly dug earth, so close the toes of his shoes sank into it a little. He stooped to tug a card out from beneath a bruised-looking lily but the paper was soggy and the writing blurred. He tried another, attached to a rather austere garland of white roses, and this time made out, "My Darling Husband." Had Kaufman married again? Or had that gaunt wife who'd watched Christophe's father being laid on her sofa somehow outlived him? Surely that was impossible. That letter he'd found, a doctor urging Kaufman to bring his wife to him before the disease progressed, that under no circumstances was another pregnancy to be attempted, that whatever embarrassment he or his wife might experience was immaterial when her life, finally, was at stake. The sort of language he'd overheard his own father use: *serious consequences, ultimately fatal, embarrassment is no defense against disease.* Was it syphilis? He'd often thought so.

The workman had finished with the spade. He carried it off to a small doorway at the rear of the church, and when he came back he gave Christophe a nod. "Is it the one you're looking for then?"

"I don't know."

The man picked up a folded tarpaulin from next to the fence, but it was wet and slipped in his hands. Something fell to the ground. He swore and grabbed it up, and Christophe thought for a moment it was a white stick before his brain let him understand: a bone. The man saw him staring and held it out but Christophe shook his head. "Ground's full of them," the man said. "Can't dig a grave here without digging up someone else." He gave a quick laugh. "People think the church is sinking into the ground—it's not that, it's the ground rising up from all these people we keep burying.

Church has been here for over seven hundred years. Imagine, thousands of them piled on top of each other and turned to dirt." He laughed again and shook his head as though it were the best joke in the world.

The rain was coming down harder now. Christophe stared at the mud dimpling where the drops landed. He wished away the gnawing pressure in his bladder but it was all he could think about, and it would come back to him when he went to sleep that night, that tight, prickling feeling and how he'd relieved himself against the fence while the rain pounded down on the grave beside him, and in his dreams it was his piss raining down, washing away the mud to reveal a humerus, a sternum, a cranium with a grinning row of teeth, all of it crawling with tiny white creatures that had eaten away the flesh and one day would eat away his too. He'd started out of that nightmare and queasily batted at his undershirt, then he'd stared through the darkness, scratching himself over and over.

MATT MORTON

Ars Poetica with Watermark

Strange things are happening in the sky again.
A stork is performing figure-eights,
dangling an anvil on fishing line from its beak.
The afternoon sun rubs shoulders with the moon.
A giant pair of scissors is slicing up
the origami clouds, the remnants of which filter down
like factory ash, coating the shiny hoods of SUVs
in the overflow lots. Would you feel more at home
if I said this was all a dream? If you'd like, you can ask
that white tiger loitering on the corner
what we're all doing here on the strange side of town.
Try to make sense of things. Believe me, I know the feeling
of chasing a soccer ball down an alley, only to realize
you've forgotten which house was yours,
and it doesn't seem so long ago that you left
your magnifying glass beside an anthill,
traded in your old records for a list
of esoteric synonyms. Still, I don't understand it—
this obsession with pinning yourself down on a map.
It's funny, when you think about it.
As if you could rectify your situation
simply by naming where you are,
or get in the ocean's good graces by measuring
all the rain we've had this year.

ALEXANDRA TEAGUE

Matryoshka (as Madness)

If you could start
at the center: nest
a solid self inside
a safer self
like a house
so no one sees
all the ways you've
twisted open, copied
yourself. How you
don't knock down
the nesting wasps
from your back porch
eves, the yard guarded
by copies of medieval
devils: their buzz
beautiful and maybe
deadly if a child knocks.
You are supposed to
make your home safe,
supposed to know dishes
from devil, but you still
throw plates for
their beautiful shatter
when it's all too solid
or isn't. Houses burn
quick as the air
between bodies.
It scares you to know this.
To know so little
of how to throw your self
into adulthood
like a voice.
The one solid wood

doll is the smallest:
trapped inside wood
inside air inside wood
like a prayer in a crucifix
you don't know how to
believe in. The church
only solid as
the ripped-roofed blue
the congregation
stares into in Siquieros,
their prayers like a windbreak:
pale trees in the sure belief
of storm. Above,
the devil hovers:
arms like a combine,
thrashing, threshing
their stares. It's best not
to look up when the sky
opens, sure of
nothing but opening.
Maybe all bodies
are storms, hurricanes
twisting up from
water, thrashing inside
them whatever else
you are. Your nephew
breaks down, breaks
open his house, is
wrestled into handcuffs,
locked up for safety.
A doll inside the body
of a glass-eyed doll.
Who would you ask for
if you called? Glass
shattered on your
floor, as if you're
trying to lock yourself
inside his mind.
Just south of him,
in Mexico, rising crime

means rising calls
for exorcisms. To unlock
the soul from the devil
like a knot pulled
from wood. The priests
say people summon evil
by praying to skulls.
Everyone praying
to their own hollows.

Tabloid Elegy

"The suicide of this attractive American girl adds another name
to the list of many women of refinement, breeding and culture
who have in recent years come to a shocking end through disre-
gard of the fundamental law of morality . . . and an immoderate
love of luxury and gayety."   —*The American Weekly*, 1921

In the page-count of death, you're a scant halfway:
your string of pearls swung, innocent as a jump rope,

to the fold. As if you were still a child at a game
of Double Dutch. Skip: sidewalk and sky. Skip: Paris

and bathtub gin. Skip: virtue. Stockings on the radiator, legs bare
as new neon tubes. How could you know the charming host

meant you when he said "dancing girls"? Said "entertainment."
His accent bristled softly like cloves piercing an orange:

a pomander hanging in a room you kept entering
a little dizzy. What's that he said about the seven veils?

You liked the new revolving doors. How it felt to spin
in a storm of your own making. Who cared Van Kannel invented them

because he didn't like to hold the door for ladies? Skip:
being a lady. Skip: being there at all. Those pillows like satin

lamps. Iridescence burning into morning. You should have been able
to wash off anything in all those fountains. How could you know

the fundamental law of doors—the ones that keep opening
keep closing behind you? Right below your breasts:

more florid headlines—*Choir Girl Ruined
By Hate. Italian Chef Sued for Serving Queer Prunes. Why*

Mrs. Halley Peck Had to Kill Herself—skip
no humiliations. *Crashed Balloonist Lives by Eating Pigeons.*

L. S. KLATT

Lost Dialect

I wish to be alive under my hat, & mouth off like a crow, a blue-eyed blackbird in a sequoia. I would speak my mind to other crows, crowds in a blue sky. Knowing that each creature has its own ideas, I would let my fellows cache their theories and fake cache. And when one crow to my own throes would succumb, I would gather around it, then leave silently en route to the database, crownless in a data cloud.

Original Mule

The river waits for the monologue of a pink tongue. The darkness is oasis. It invites sightseeing, though there is a decided absence of moonlight. As the tongue approaches, what does it see? Does it see opaquely that there are coal-fire power plants & a night of star anise, oblong boats & a myrrh sunrise? The tongue ventures out into sepia vapors where a mule flicks extravagant ears, & conifers along the sable river char. How could we not want the mule, the original mule cut whole cloth out of feeling? It sashays decoratively in a stride that will not be parsed among exuberant leaves. The fashionable ass shifts its burden, happier in work than we tired tailors deserve; whatever is felt has survived our nimble shears.

MICHAEL LEE

A History of the Knife

The knife is envious of bones, each metatarsal
of the foot, collar and jaw, but especially

the rib, and its motionless rest. The knife,
remembers when it was bone, when it lived

inside an elk, or man, and kept the rind
together until it didn't, until the body was used to cut

the body from itself. Do you see how everything returns
to its maker? The way an elephant remembers, perfectly,

and returns to where it once rose like grey light
from the earth-its bones cutting through

the hide-a sculpture of moonlight unearthed
by the sharp arms of the clock as they swing

at the flank. The sunlight enters, guiding the flies,
and their rhythmless chatter as if death were a kind

of waking, a realization the body has.
Where else do you expect the knife to go

other than back inside us? Here, beside the heart,
where it sleeps like a tucked wing. A loose bone.

A lever which undoes the skeleton
when pulled. Here, the heart, a darkened rind,

its humming blood hot and lit
like a cinder. The knife must believe this dark

cage of bones to be the cave
in which it first was formed.

The pulse, a steady swinging of stone
sharpening its edge.

J. CAMP BROWN

Femur | Flute

In the mouth of the wolf, that socket
   of hunger, is a circumduction of
      bone:—rubble

dug up from a thin gravel
   pall, marrow of which
      gunks yellow

the growl-spit and muzzle. The bitch
   slops drool and flees.
      Fire made man

man? No:—in the beginning is this
   limb picked clean and
      punctured, this

mother's sob:—it brads a hole:—
   this bone that flutes back
      her hollow howl.

GARY HAWKINS

Ode to the Tick

Flattened wish, sentinel
of empty lots, daemon of pine barrens
even after fire walls the bark,
you embody implicit faith
in bodies—a dot only for your own.
Patience for some is hours: months
you wait for a chance to drop,
pest who learned from the locusts
about the steadfastness of Job.
No route through the salt meadow
can miss you, no vein
can break your cold vector.
No, Vigilance, you are intimate
of all of my folds.
A freckle in a warm spot
that is new—Little Other,
pollinator, blood sucker,
my fever, my poison.
Not even fate comes as silently as you.

ELIZABETH BRADFIELD

Emperor Penguins at Snow Hill Island

All week, emails flung to satellites, slung down, ship to ship—seen here. For once, the Weddell open to latitude, day scheduled ours, clear & calm. Approached pack. All eyes on deck, binos keeping distance less distant. Who spots them? H? E? Not me. Then almost too easy, too plain

tall hunch at ice-edge
no brilliance at throat, beak
closer, brilliant

Thinking of Cherry, his first by moonlight & aurora. Don't go inside for offered coffee, biscuits. Or to skype this (if reception, if time on the purchased card). Sea ice bumps to horizon, last year's shuffling tabulars trapped in old pack. Connected, apart. Why are we here? Decadence. Delight. Desire. A tourist ship discovered this colony just ten years ago. Discovered. Could have been us. Could have.

Here/Elsewhere

At sea. Horizon & albatross. Stern wake & petrel. So many so many such soaring. Or the same few. Hard to say. In news: birds drawn by longline bait, hooked, pulled into deep, deepest plunge. Or Polyethylene shredded to chum, plucked from wave crest, flown to nest, voided into chick gape as food. & thus what lasts: plastic-gut carcasses, feather & bone fading around bright center.

> albatross circle
> a cockeyed feather marks one
> allows one reckoning

Later, alone on deck with tea. Travel mug from home set on rail. A swell. Skitter & rattle—gone. This message of our passage, of what I carry.

Aitcho Islands

Sneeze of a place, "officially unnamed" scrawl we scope & wander. Tide ebbs. The landing complicates to serrations each boat must weave. Easier to stay offshore until called, lounge, feet up on the port pontoon, until breeze pushes to danger, pulls to steer away.

old ice drifts in
five crabeaters nap on crumble
seals, berg scarred

If quiet, if low, if unsudden, an approach. Clutch ahead to north edge, drift the face. Ice red with krill-shit, chill sun burrows that darkness to melt. All five scarred, old tracks deep on flank & belly so long past source that none nurse them, none startle the flinch of the once-got. A female stretches foreflipper, eyes closed. Past, I recognize you.

PAMELA ALEXANDER

Easter Island

Strangers on wooden islands
brought beads and knives. And hats!

We snatched them off heads
and they called us *thieves*.

Then they made sickness
so that many of us died.

Our forest sickened too,
the fat palms dwindling.

We measured the ships
with string, with steps, made

prayer huts that size
to call the new powers.

Built mounds of earth
with narrow ends, dug moats

around them, put up
poles and cloth.

More ships. From them ran
small animals with pink tails

that multiplied like ships
and ate saplings and seeds.

We couldn't kill enough of them.
We did what we could: sailed

our dirt decks, sang to the sky
and to our stone gods.

Still the forest left us.
Now we are few.

Strangers in metal boats
bring a little money

and tell us our bare island
is talked about in many places

and we're famous for this:
killing all our trees.

G. C. WALDREP

Easterhouse (Wyoming)

Sometimes within the natural, a little love is heard.
Called blind, neither touch nor voice
stood in the close　　　　of history's gnashed flesh:
the golden hair of language, its shadow-verb

laid to rest in wheat-throat, music's compact fret.
I felt a fragrant dusk skimming the green
away, my love like a garment of bone, a winter-skin
held as neither instrument nor breath—

a mesh made new through cession, blue & naked.
I stormed God's body like a black thread.
Death went around
to touch each soul, little bride, spitaling night-fire.

What people buy in dreams
weakens me: burnt honey, sleeping
meat-machines, those sparrows / approached as bell
even as the forest stitches its last green candle.

Light my way now, brother-body.
I linger at the glass gate
in the shadow of God's vast flaming dare
where my children, each quelled debt, once played.

Bios

PAMELA ALEXANDER has published four collections of poems, including *Slow Fire* (Ausable/Copper Canyon, 2007). Her nonfiction has recently appeared in *Cimarron Review* and *Denver Quarterly*. She taught creative writing for many years at M.I.T. and Oberlin College and is on the editorial board of *FIELD* magazine.

JASWINDER BOLINA is the author of *Phantom Camera* (New Issues, 2013) winner of the Green Rose Prize in Poetry, and *Carrier Wave* (Center for Literary Publishing, 2007), winner of the 2006 Colorado Prize for Poetry. His latest collection is a digital chapbook, *The Tallest Building in America*, now available online at floatingwolfquarterly.com. He teaches at the University of Miami.

CHARLIE BONDHUS' second book of poetry, *All the Heat We Could Carry*, won the 2013 Main Street Rag Award and the 2014 Thom Gunn Award for Gay Poetry. His work appears in numerous journals, including *The Bellevue Literary Review*, *CounterPunch*, *The Gay & Lesbian Review*, and *Poetry*. He teaches at Raritan Valley Community College and is the poetry editor at *The Good Men Project*.

ELIZBETH BRADFIELD is the author of three poetry collections: *Once Removed* (Persea, 2015), *Approaching Ice* (2010), and *Interpretive Work* (Arktoi Books/Red Hen, 2008). Her work has appeared widely, including in *Atlantic Monthly*, *Field*, *The New Yorker*, *Poetry* and elsewhere. She is the Jacob Ziskind Visiting Poet-in-Residence at Brandeis and teaches in the low-residency MFA program at the University of Alaska, Anchorage.

GERRI BRIGHTWELL is the author of the novels *Dead of Winter* (Salt Publishing, 2016; forthcoming), *The Dark Lantern* (Three Rivers Press, 2009), and *Cold Country* (Bristol Classical Press, 2003). Her writing has also appeared (or is forthcoming) in such venues as BBC Radio Four's *Opening Lines*, *Gargoyle*, *Los Angeles Review*, *Redivider*, and elsewhere. She teaches at the University of Alaska, Fairbanks.

J. CAMP BROWN is a bluegrass mandolinist hailing from Fort Smith, AR. He has received fellowships from the Arkansas Arts Council and Phillips Exeter Academy. His poems have recently appeared in *Crazyhorse*, *Booth*, *Front Porch*, *Memorious*, and elsewhere. He teaches English in Poughkeepsie, NY.

CHRISTOPHER BRUNT is a poet and fiction writer whose work appears in *Bat City Review*, *Drunken Boat*, *Ploughshares*, and elsewhere. He teaches literature for the University of Houston Honors College and holds both an MFA from Syracuse and a PhD from the University of Southern Mississippi. He is currently at work on a novel.

CATHY LINH CHE is the author of the poetry collection *Split* (Alice James Books, 2014), winner of the Kundiman Poetry Prize and the Norma Farber First Book Award from the Poetry Society of America.

JESSA CRISPIN is editor-in-chief of the litblog/webzine *Bookslut*, founded in 2002. Her writing has appeared in *The Washington Post, The Chicago Sun-Times, The Guardian, The Toronto Globe and Mail,* and elsewhere. She lives in Chicago. "The Self-Hating Book Critic" is forthcoming in the book, *Literary Publishing in the Twenty-First Century.*

ASHLEY DAVIDSON's stories have appeared in *Five Chapters, Nashville Review, Shenandoah, Sou'wester,* and other journals. She holds an MFA from the Iowa Writers' Workshop and lives in Flagstaff, Arizona.

Among the most renowned Turkish poets born in the mid-20th century, **HAYDAR ERGÜLEN** has published more than a dozen books and received numerous national prizes for his work. For more information, see page 65.

ELYSE FENTON is the author of the poetry collections *Clamor* (Cleveland State UP, 2010) and *Sweet Insurgent* (Saturnalia Books, forthcoming).

In addition to many books of poems, several anthologies, and a collection of stories, **STUART FRIEBERT** has published, among his eleven volumes of translations, three editions of Karl Krolow's Selected Poems, most recently *Karl Krolow's Puppets in the Wind* (Bitter Oleander Press, 2014).

JANE FRIEDMAN has 20 years of experience in the publishing industry, with expertise in digital media strategy. She is a former editor with the *Virginia Quarterly Review* and a columnist for *Publishers Weekly.* Jane currently teaches at the University of Virginia. She has spoken at events such as BookExpo America, Digital Book World, and the AWP Conference, and has served on panels with the National Endowment for the Arts. "The Future Value of a Literary Publisher" is forthcoming in the book *Literary Publishing in the Twenty-First Century.*

MARILYN HACKER is the author of thirteen books of poems, including *A Stranger's Mirror* (Norton, 2015) and *Names* (2010), an essay collection, *Unauthorized Voices* (Univ of Michigan Press, 2010), and thirteen collections of translations of French and Francophone poets. *DiaspoRenga,* written in collaboration with Deema Shehabi, was published by Holland Park Press in 2014. Her awards include the Lenore Marshall Prize, two Lambda Literary Awards, the PEN award for poetry in translation, the PEN Voelcker Award and the international Argana Prize for Poetry from the Beit as-Sh'ir/ House of Poetry in Morocco. She lives in Paris.

GARY HAWKINS' debut collection of poetry is *Worker* (Main Street Rag, 2016). His poetry, pedagogy, and criticism have appeared in *Forklift: Ohio*, *Emily Dickinson Journal*, *Los Angeles Review of Books*, and elsewhere. With his wife, the poet Landon Godfrey, he edits and produces *Croquet*, an occasional letterpress postcard broadside.

HENRY ISRAELI's upcoming collection, *god's breath hovering across the waters*, will be published by Four Way Books in 2016. He is the translator of *Haywire: New and Selected Poems* (Bloodaxe, 2011), *Child of Nature* (New Directions, 2010), and *Fresco: The Selected Poetry of Luljeta Lleshanaku* (2002), as well as the founder and editor of Saturnalia Books. He teaches at Drexel University.

DAVID KEPLINGER is the author of four collections of poetry and three volumes in translation from the Danish and the German, and he has written and recorded a roots music album, *By & By*, based on the poetry of his great-great grandfather, a veteran of the Union Army. His most recent collection is *The Most Natural Thing* (New Issues, 2013).

New poems from **L. S. KLATT** have appeared recently in *Gulf Coast*, *Harvard Review*, *The Iowa Review*, *VOLT*, and elsewhere. His third collection of poetry, *Sunshine Wound*, was published by Free Verse Editions (Parlor Press) in 2014. He is the current Poet Laureate of Grand Rapids, Michigan.

KARL KROLOW, revered by many as one of a handful of Germany's very best poets of the 20th century, published more than thirty volumes of poetry and authored numerous books of prose, translations, and criticism. For more on Krolow, see page 121.

ALICIA LAI is the Founder and Editor-in-chief of *The Postscript Journal*, an international in-print literary magazine. A YoungArts National Winner and a U.S. Presidential Scholar in the Arts, she recently won the Easterday Poetry Prize from the National Poetry Quarterly. Her work appears in *Curio Poetry*, *The Kenyon Review*, and *Lascaux Review*, and has been featured at the Smithsonian Institute and the Kennedy Center for the Performing Arts. She attends Princeton University.

MICHAEL LEE is a Norwegian-American writer and author of the chapbook *Secondly. Finally* (Organic Weapon Arts, 2014), which was selected by Natalie Diaz for the 2014 David Blair Memorial Prize. Having received grants from the Minnesota State Arts Board, the Loft Literary Center, and the Metropolitan Regional Arts Council, his work appears in *Hayden's Ferry Review*, *Indiana Review*, *Ninth Letter*, *Phoebe*, and elsewhere. He attends the Harvard Graduate School of Education.

Originally from Zimbabwe, **BERNARD FARAI MATAMBO** has published work in *AGNI, Cincinnati Review, Pleiades, Witness,* and elsewhere. He has also received numerous awards for his work, including fellowships from the Blue Mountain Center and the I-Park Foundation, the 2013 Walter Rumsey Marvin Grant awarded by the Ohioana Library to the most promising writer under thirty, and an international arts education grant from the Minneapolis Foundation to develop community arts and arts education in Zimbabwe. Matambo teaches at Oberlin College.

DERICK MATTERN is a poet and translator who lived and worked in Istanbul from 2008-13. His translations of Haydar Ergülen's work appear in *Guernica, Gulf Coast,* and *Modern Poetry in Translation.*

MARC McKEE's poetry collections are *Bewilderness* (Black Lawrence Press, 2014) and *Fuse* (2011), as well as the chapbook *What Apocalypse?*, which won the New Michigan Press/DIAGRAM 2008 Chapbook Contest. His work has appeared recently in *Forklift, OH; inter|rupture; Memorious; The Laurel Review;* and the Academy of American Poets Poem-a-day. He teaches at the University of Missouri at Columbia, where he lives with his wife, Camellia Cosgray, and their son, Harold.

MATT MORTON's poems appear in *Gulf Coast, Indiana Review, Quarterly West, West Branch,* and elsewhere. He has been a finalist both for a Ruth Lilly Fellowship and in the *Narrative Magazine* 30 Below Story and Poetry Contest. Recently, Bob Hicok selected his poem "Windfall" as the winner of the *Sycamore Review* 2014 Wabash Prize for Poetry.

LAUREN MOSELEY's poems have recently appeared in *The Journal, Mississippi Review, Narrative Magazine, Pleiades,* and the anthologies *Best New Poets* and *Women Write Resistance.* She has been a recipient of an artist's grant from the Money for Women/Barbara Deming Memorial Fund, a finalist for the Writers @ Work Fellowship Competition, and a resident at the Virginia Center for the Creative Arts. She lives in Durham, North Carolina.

The author of twelve poetry collections, **EMMANUEL MOSES** was born in Casablanca in 1959. A collection of his poems translated by Marilyn Hacker was published in 2009 by the Oberlin College Press FIELD Translation Series. For more about Moses, see page 27.

SEQUOIA NAGAMATSU is the author of the forthcoming story collection, *Where We Go When All We Were Is Gone* (Black Lawrence Press, 2016). His stories have recently appeared in *Conjunctions*, The *Fairy Tale Review*, *Puerto Del Sol*, and *Tin House* online, among others. He is the managing editor of *Psychopomp Magazine* and a visiting assistant professor at The College of Idaho.

JOHN O'BRIEN founded the *Review of Contemporary Fiction in 1981,* Dalkey Archive Press in 1984, and *CONTEXT* magazine in 1999. "19 Things: more thoughts on the future of fiction" is forthcoming in the book *Literary Publishing in the Twenty-First Century.*

A. G. PERRY is a PhD student in Literature and Creative Writing at the University of Houston, where she also serves as the current editor of *Gulf Coast.* She is a Kimbilio Fellow, has work forthcoming in *Indiana Review*, and is currently at work on both a novel and a collection of short stories.

MAGGIE QUEENEY reads and writes in Chicago. Her recent work has appeared in *Handsome, Packingtown Review, The Southeast Review*, and *Southern Poetry Review.*

DEAN RADER's poetry collections are *Self-Portrait as Wikipedia Entry* (Copper Canyon, 2016; forthcoming), *Landscape Portrait Figure Form* (Omnidawn, 2013), and *Works & Days* (Truman State UP, 2010). He teaches at the University of San Francisco.

JACQUES J. RANCOURT's poems have appeared in *The Kenyon Review, New England Review, Ploughshares, Virginia Quarterly Review,* and *Best New Poets 2014.* He's held fellowships and residencies from the Stegner program at Stanford University, the Wisconsin Institute for Creative Writing, and at the Cité Internationale des Arts in Paris, France.

ANDREA READ was born in Rochester, New York, and has earned degrees from Rice University, University of Chicago and Lesley University. A recipient of a National Resource Fellowship and a Tinker Foundation Grant, she has taught Spanish and Latin American literature and language at Columbia College, Beloit College, The University of Chicago, and Stanford University. Her poems have appeared in *The Painted Bride Quarterly, Third Bed*, and are forthcoming in *FIELD.* Andrea resides in Somerville, Massachusetts.

RACHEL RICHARDSON's poetry collections are *Hundred-Year Wave* (Carnegie Mellon Poetry, 2016; forthcoming) and *Copperhead* (2011). The recipient of NEA and Wallace Stegner Fellowships, as well as the Hopwood Award and five Dorothy Sargent Rosenberg Prizes, she lives in Berkeley, CA.

WESLEY ROTHMAN's poems appear in *32 Poems, Harvard Review, New England Review, Prairie Schooner*, and elsewhere. His criticism appears in *Boston Review, Rain Taxi*, and *American Microreviews and Interviews*. He teaches writing and cultural literatures throughout Boston.

LYNDA SEXSON's work appears in recent issues of *Epoch, The Gettysburg Review, The Kenyon Review, The Literary Review*, and elsewhere. Her books are *Hamlet's Planets: Parables* (Ohio State UP, 1996), *Ordinarily Sacred* (Univ of Virginia Press, 1992), and *Margaret of the Imperfections*, (Persea Books, 1989).

ROB STEPHENS is a PhD student at Florida State University. His work has previously appeared in *Cream City Review, Epoch, Lake Effect, Minnesota Review*, and others. Rob lives in Tallahassee with his wife, Jaclyn Dwyer, and their daughter.

ALEXANDRA TEAGUE is the author of two books of poetry: *The Wise and Foolish Builders* (Persea Books, 2015) and *Mortal Geography* (2010), winner of the 2009 Lexi Rudnitsky Prize and the 2010 California Book Award for Poetry. The recipient of a Stegner Fellowship, a National Endowment for the Arts Fellowship, and the 2014 *Missouri Review* Editors' Prize, Teague teaches at the University of Idaho and is an editor for Broadsided Press.

G. C. WALDREP is the author most recently of *Testament* (BOA Editions, 2015) and a chapbook, *Susquehanna* (Omnidawn, 2013). He lives in Lewisburg, PA, where he teaches at Bucknell University, edits the journal *West Branch*, and serves as Editor-at-Large for *The Kenyon Review*.

MICHAEL VAN WALLEGHEN is Professor Emeritus of Creative Writing at the University of Illinois at Urbana-Champaign. He won the Lamont Award in 1980 for his collection *More Trouble with the Obvious* and has won two NEA grants, a Pushcart Prize, and the Borestone Mountain Poetry Prize. He has published six books of poetry and is presently working on another collection.

Required Reading

(Issue 22)

(Each issue we ask that our contributors recommend up to three recent titles. What follows is the list generated by this issue's contributors.)

Patience Agbabi, *Telling Tales* (Marilyn Hacker)

Daniel Alarcón, *At Night We Walk in Circles* (Michael Lee)

Lynda Barry, *What It Is* (Elizabeth Bradfield)

Quan Barry, *Loose Strife* (Jacques J. Rancourt)

Svetislav Basara, *Fata Morgana*, trans. Ronald Major (John O'Brien)

Nicky Beer, *The Octopus Game* (Marc McKee)

Best European Fiction, preface by Jon Fosse (John O'Brien)

Michael Bhaskar, *The Content Machine* (Jane Friedman)

Judith Bowles, *The Gatherer* (David Keplinger)

Anne Boyer, *Garments Against Women* (Jessa Crispin)

Ta-Nehisi Coates, *Between the World and Me* (Christopher Brunt, Michael Lee)

Collins, Prufer, & Rock, eds. *Catherine Breese Davis: On the Life & Work of an American Master* (Michael Van Walleghen)

Tim Early, *Poems Descriptive of Rural Life and Scenery* (J. Camp Brown)

Carrie Fountain, *Instant Winner* (Rachel Richardson)

Karen Joy Fowler, *We Are All Completely Beside Ourselves* (Lynda Sexson)

Angela Flournoy, *The Turner House* (Lauren Moseley)

John Gallaher, *In a Landscape* (Matt Morton)

William H. Gass, *Life Sentences* (John O'Brien)

Ross Gay, *Catalogue of Unabashed Gratitude* (Cathy Linh Che, Gary Hawkins, Henry Israeli)

Amy Gerstler, *Scattered at Sea* (Henry Israeli)

Lauren Haldeman, *Calenday* (Ashley Davidson)

Judy Halebsky, *Tree Line* (Dean Rader)

Barbara Hamby, *On the Street of Divine Love: New & Selected Poems* (Rob Stephens)

Gail Hareven, *Lies, First Person*, trans. Dalya Bilu (Jessa Crispin)

Brian Hart, *The Bully of Order* (Ashley Davidson)

Matthea Harvey, *If the Tabloids Are True What Are You* (Gary Hawkins)

Tatsumi Hijikata, *Costume en Face: A Primer of Darkness for Young Boys and Girls*, trans. Sawako Nakayasu (G. C. Waldrep)

Cynthia Marie Hoffman, *Paper Doll Fetus* (Alexandra Teague)

Richie Hofmann, *Second Empire* (Matt Morton)

Chloe Honum, *The Tulip-Flame* (Matt Morton)

Major Jackson, *Roll Deep* (Derick Mattern)

Amaud Jamaul Johnson, *Darktown Follies* (J. Camp Brown)

Tim Johnston, *Descent* (Lauren Moseley)

Mimi Khalvati, *The Weather Wheel* (Marilyn Hacker)

Paul Kingsborth, *The Wake* (Gerri Brightwell)

Austin Kleon, *Show Your Work* (Jane Friedman)

Dean Kostos, *This Is Not a Skyscraper* (Charlie Bondhus)

Julia Kristeva, *Teresa, My Love: An Imagined Life of the Saint of Avila*, trans. Lorna Scott Fox (Jessa Crispin)

Rachel Kushner, *The Flame-Throwers* (Christopher Brunt)

Eugenia Leighs, *Sparrows, Blood and Blood* (Elyse Fenton)

Robin Coste Lewis, *Voyage of the Sable Venus* (A. G. Perry)

Nicholas Lovell, *The Curve* (Jane Friedman)

James Lovelock, *A Rough Ride into the Future* (Stuart Friebert)

Valeria Luiselli, *The Story of My Teeth*, trans. Christina MacSweeney (Lynda Sexson)

Helen Macdonald, *H Is for Hawk* (Pamela Alexander)

George Makari, *Soul Machine: The Invention of the Modern Mind* (Michael Van Walleghen)

Emily St. John Mandel, *Station Eleven* (Gerri Brightwell)

Jynne Dilling Martin, *We Mammals in Hospitable Times* (Rachel Richardson)

Cate Marvin, *Oracle* (Andrea Read)

Tom McCarthy, *Satin Island* (Lynda Sexson)

Shane McCrae, *The Animal Too Big to Kill* (Wesley Rothman)

Jane Mead, *Money Money Money Water Water Water* (Pamela Alexander)

Tessa Mellas, *Lungs Full of Noise* (Sequoia Nagamatsu)

Philip Metres, *Sand Opera* (Marilyn Hacker)

Andrew Milward, *I Was a Revolutionary* (Christopher Brunt)

Susanna Mishler, *Termination Dust* (Alexandra Teague)

Lenelle Moïse, *Haiti Glass* (Charlie Bondhus)

Jenny Molberg, *Marvels of the Invisible* (David Keplinger)

Haruki Murakami, *Colorless Tsukuru Tazaki and His Years of Pilgrimage*, trans. Philip Gabriel (Lynda Sexson)

Jay Nebel, *Neighbors* (Elyse Fenton)

Hieu Minh Nguyen, *This Way to Sugar* (Cathy Linh Che)

Geoffrey Nutter, *The Rose of January* (L. S. Klatt)

Matthew Olzmann, *Mezzanines* (Jaswinder Bolina)

Ahmatjan Osman, *Uyghurland, the Furthest Exile*, trans. Jeffrey Yang (Derick Mattern)

Ladan Osman, *The Kitchen-Dweller's Testimony* (Wesley Rothman)

Ruth Ozeki, *A Tale for the Time Being* (Cathy Linh Che)

Kevin Prufer, *Churches* (Andrea Read)

Claudia Rankine, *Citizen* (Elizabeth Bradfield, Michael Lee)

Rita Mae Reese, *The Book of Hulga* (Alexandra Teague)

Carl Safina, *Beyond Words: What Animals Think and Feel* (Stuart Friebert)

Chika Sagawa, *Collected Poems*, trans. Sawako Nakayasu (G. C. Waldrep)

Elizabeth Savage, *Idylliad* (Dean Rader)

Julie Schumacher, *Dear Committee Members* (Stuart Friebert)

Maureen Seaton, *Fibonacci Batman* (Jaswinder Bolina)

Lee Sharkey, *Calendars of Fire* (Jacques J. Rancourt)

Evie Shockley, *The new black* (Jaswinder Bolina)

Sandra Simonds, *Steal It Back* (Henry Israeli)

Ali Smith, *How to Be Both* (Gerri Brightwell)

Juliana Spahr, *That Winter the Wolf Came* (Charlie Bondhus)

Frank Stanford, *What About This: Collected Poems of Frank Stanford* (Marc McKee)

Mary Szybist, *Incarnadine* (Gary Hawkins)

Wislawa Szymborska, *Map*, trans. Clare Cavanagh (Michael Van Walleghen)

Sam Taylor, *Nude Descending an Empire* (David Keplinger)

Anne Valente, *By Light We Knew Our Names* (Sequoia Nagamatsu)

José Ángel Valente, *Landscape with Yellow Birds*, trans. Thomas Christensen (Andrea Read)

Jean Valentine, *Shirt in Heaven* (Lauren Moseley)

Ellen Bryant Voigt, *Headwaters* (Jacques J. Rancourt)

Orlando White, *LETTERRS* (Dean Rader)

Dara Wier, *You Good Thing* (L. S. Klatt)

Emily Wilson, *The Great Medieval Yellows* (Pamela Alexander)

Dennis Wood, *Everything Sings: Maps for a Narrative Atlas* (G. C. Waldrep)

Jeff Wood, *The Glacier* (Sequoia Nagamatsu)

Stephanie Wortman, *In the Permanent Collection* (Marc McKee)

Jake Adam York, *Abide* (Wesley Rothman)

Alexi Zentner, *The Lobster Kings* (Ashley Davidson)

Nell Zink, *The Wallcreeper* (Elizabeth Bradfield)

The Copper Nickel Editors' Prizes
(est. 2015)

(Two $500 prizes awarded to the most exciting work published in the issue, as determined by a vote of the Copper Nickel staff)

Past Winners

fall 2015 (issue 21)

Jonathan Weinert, poetry
Tyler Mills, prose

spring 2015 (issue 20)

Michelle Oakes, poetry
Donovan Ortega, prose

the *JOURNAL*

a literary magazine

SUBMIT

WWW.THEJOURNALMAG.ORG

POETRY

FICTION

NONFICTION

REVIEWS

ART

Winter • 2016

Announcing

THE
JAKE ADAM YORK PRIZE
for a first or second poetry collection

coordinated by
COPPER NICKEL

the winning book will be published by
MILKWEED EDITIONS

with
$2,000 + a standard royalty contract

manuscripts due:
October 15, 2016

final judge:
ROSS GAY

submission fee: $25

all entrants will receive a year's subscription
to COPPER NICKEL

for more info visit:
copper-nickel.org/bookprize/

COPPERNICKEL

subscription rates

For regular folks:

one year (two issues)—$20
two years (four issues)—$35
three years (six issues)—$45
five years (ten issues)—$60

For student folks:

one year (two issues)—$15
two years (four issues)—$23
three years (six issues)—$32
five years (ten issues)—$50

For more information, visit: www.copper-nickel.org.

To go directly to subscriptions
visit: www.regonline.com/coppernickelsubscriptions.

To order back issues, call 303-556-4026
or email wayne.miller@ucdenver.edu.